EROTIC
COMICS

VOLUME 2

EROTIC COMICS

A GRAPHIC HISTORY

VOLUME 2
FROM THE 1970s TO THE PRESENT DAY

Tim Pilcher
Foreword by Alan Moore

ILEX

First published in the United Kingdom in 2008 by

I L E X

The Old Candlemakers
West Street
Lewes
East Sussex BN7 2NZ
www.ilex-press.com

This book was conceived by:
ILEX
Cambridge
England

Publisher: Alastair Campbell
Creative Director: Peter Bridgewater
Managing Editor: Chris Gatcum
Senior Editor: Adam Juniper
Art Director: Julie Weir
Designer: Jonathan Raimes

British Library Cataloguing-in-Publication Data
A catalogue record for this book is available from
the British Library.

ISBN 978-1905814-37-4

Printed and bound in Thailand

For more information on this title please visit:
www.web-linked.com/erc2uk

Previous page:
A hentai-inspired Wongoboy painting
by British artist Jason Atomic.

Right:
A Vaughn Bodé original reworked by
his son Mark for SF Surfboards.

CONTENTS

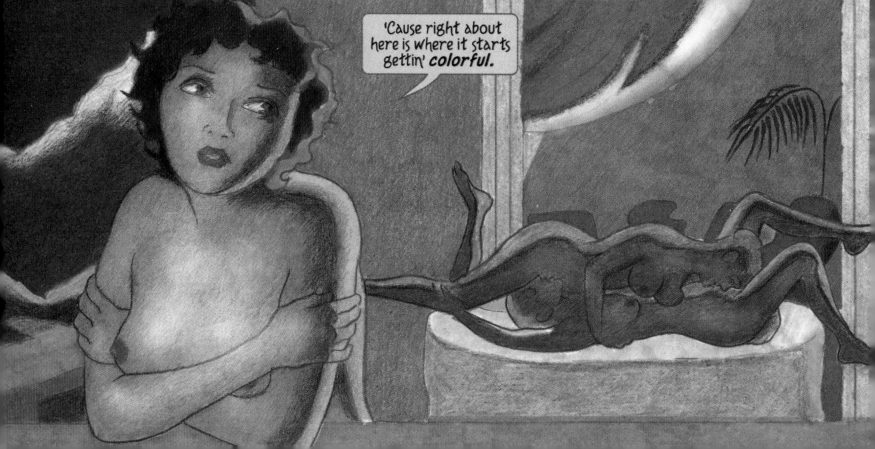

FOREWORD: DRAWINGS OF HARLOTS

Pornography—from the Greek *pórnë* or harlot, plus *graphos*, to draw or to write—is an impulse as old as mankind. We encountered it during our cultural infancy, crouched in our caves with a Willendorf Venus for company, and it was there during our individual childhoods, scrawled in hurried ballpoint on lavatory walls or buried in poorly delivered and confusing dirty jokes at playtime. Even then, behind the bike sheds, we were made aware that even if we didn't really understand them, these were narratives best not repeated to our parents. These were routines that could get us into trouble, although what variety of trouble wasn't made entirely clear. Perhaps it boiled down to "What if your mother heard you tell that story? What if she found that dog-eared copy of *The Carpetbaggers* that always falls open at the lesbian scene? What if she came across the dirty picture that you did?" Essentially, "What if somebody like your mother, someone decent, knew that you had sexual thoughts and a developing sexual identity? What then?"

And so we moderate our language and reserve our bawdiness for those of our own age and gender whom we know to be as secretly depraved as we. We take on a selective furtiveness and, with it, a whole plethora of ideas and assumptions: we assume that there exists a class of people, decent people who include our parents, clergymen, and teachers in their number, who have never entertained a lewd idea in their whole lives. We furthermore assume that we ourselves number among the indecent, debased minority that is prone to such notions, and that we'd be best advised to keep them to ourselves, not realizing that this is exactly the same thing that everybody else is doing. We therefore needlessly incorporate degrees of shame into our sexual makeup, both as individuals and societies, which we may find hard to shake off, even when we know better.

The history of the church's or state's attempts to either stamp out or control erotic impulses in art is documented elsewhere and is probably best summarized by pointing out that such attempts have evidently not worked, or have worked only imperfectly: pornography is now more widespread and more prevalent than ever, and yet it is still most often both created and "enjoyed" in guilty anonymity. Effectively, we have been given an increased range of material to feel bad about, the worst of both worlds. Even so, it seems clear that the long war of attrition waged against pornography is no more winnable than is a war on terror, drugs, or any other such abstraction. The debate on whether there should be pornography or not is made irrelevant by the plain fact of its continuing existence. Legislation proving useless, this is no longer a legislative argument. We might be better off in moving the discussion onto ethical and aesthetic grounds, accepting that pornography exists and simply asking if it's any good or not, either in terms of execution or as seen from a socio-political perspective.

It strikes me that the comic medium, with its long history of involvement with erotica, has a particular advantage over other media when it comes to a successful visual depiction of the sex act: like the carefully posed nudes in a Victorian tableaux *vivant* theatrical extravaganza, figures in a comic panel are not moving. All of the inelegant—and indeed sometimes comical—contortions of the act itself can be excised, can be imagined happening somewhere between the panels, leaving only the most perfectly constructed images and moments for consideration. This allows a necessary aesthetic distance for the author and the viewer both, enabling them either to tell or to enjoy a story without the distraction of the leading man's unfortunate facial expressions or the guttural outbursts and the squelching meat percussion of the soundtrack. More importantly, since all the players are imaginary and are made from nothing except ink and paper, without need for models/actresses/whatever, then the viewer can be reassured that there is not some ugly and coercive backstory behind the leading lady's eager-to-please smile. All that we are seeing truly naked and exposed in an erotic comic story is the sexual imagination of the authors, and that, ultimately, is the only thing that we can criticize

Previous page:
Alice, Dorothy, and Wendy share an intimate moment in the final volume of Alan Moore & Melinda Gebbie's *Lost Girls* trilogy.

Left:
Melinda Gebbie's back cover design to *Lost Girls* Volume 3.

Right:
Portrait of Alan Moore by Fraizer Irvine.

or judge the work by. If a sexual idea is morbid or banal, if it is expressed poorly, let us say so without fear that we shall end up on the side of censorship, denial, or repression.

If erotica is to be taken seriously as a field, if it is to thrive and to develop, then it must become discriminating and show that it has some sort of standards; be something that we can still respect the morning after. Since all such aesthetic judgments are subjective, then by all means let us argue fiercely over where we set the bar, just as long as we all agree there is one, a dividing line that separates the works of genuine delight from those of no more value than the crumpled Kleenex that accompanied their genesis.

Within this current, beautifully presented volume it is likely that the reader will, according to his or her individual tastes, find pieces from both categories. When it comes to deciding which is which, try to be merciful and to remember that creating a graceful or satisfying pornographic work is much more difficult than it appears, perhaps because there are few good examples of the genre thus far upon which to model such a work. Pornography is very much like adolescent poetry: there's a great deal of it about because it is a very easy thing to do, and much of it is absolutely fucking dreadful because it is very hard to do it well. Please bear in mind that, being married to the exquisite Melinda

Gebbie, I have let myself become a porn-snob with impractically high standards.

With that said, the breadth of the material included should ensure that every reader is rewarded with some gem of lasting merit, if not several such. The sheer profusion of the works herein, expressed in different media and a variety of styles, suggest a thriving and, at root, a healthy field that's teeming with vitality if you can see past all the worms and the manure. For my part, I was gratified to find intelligent and generously matured offerings from long-term favorites like Howard Cruse alongside new discoveries such as the liquid, elegantly stylized forms of Jess Fink. Artists like these provide the progressive impetus that, hopefully, will allow comic strip erotica to grow and prosper in the coming century, to rise above the slurping quagmire of the *Anal Cheerleaders* home DVD, or the more dubious reaches of the Intenet with their potential for predation or entrapment. What a tangled world wide web we weave.

By way of a conclusion, I'm reminded of an incident that happened to me yesterday while I was seated in a branch of Cafe Nero (why not Cafe Heliogabalus, I often wonder, or Cafe Caligula?). A girl I knew from the nearby establishment where I purchase industrial quantities of a shampoo that promises me traffic-stopping shine and volume came into the coffee shop accompanied by her mother,

where she told me she'd just purchased a signed copy of *Lost Girls*, the pornographic marathon my wife and I have only recently completed. The young lady's mother was also effusive in her praises, being most impressed by all the splendid flourishes of the book's presentation and design. Though brief, our conversation was a pleasant, civilized example of trans-generational public discourse upon the subject of pornography that would have been unlikely to occur even five years ago. My point is that you should absorb the contents of this book, and do so shamelessly. Some of it may remind you of the toilet scribbles and unfathomable smutty playground anecdotes that were where all of us came in, but some of it is of more dazzling quality and provenance than anything which you're likely to chance upon mysteriously hidden in the bushes of your local park. You should quite clearly feel free to respond as you see fit, whether it be by laughing, retching with disgust, or simply steaming privately with your forbidden longings. And however you react, please don't worry about your mother. If I know her, she'll be getting her own copy.

Alan Moore
Northampton, UK

Left:
Italian artist Giovanna Casotto uses a limited palette in this pencil study, complementing the single use of red with subtle shades of gray, creating a sensuous and stylish illustration.

INTRODUCTION

Just like their fine-art forbearers, ever since the earliest erotic, or pornographic if you prefer, comics were published they have had to combat constant criticism and censorship. If there is a central theme to the history of erotic comics, it is the perennial struggle between freedom of expression and governmental censorship. Sexual politics is, after all, potent stuff. It forces the reader to question his or her own moral code, to reflect on society, and to question current civilization's mores and social graces, all things governments would rather their populations didn't do.

Dr. Fredric Wertham's US comic book purges of 1954, the rise and fall of the comic code, and the explosion of underground comix in the sixties and seventies saw erotic comics go through a rollercoaster of good and bad luck. The sixties' new "permissive society" unleashed a Pandora's box of erotic self-expression in sequential art that has roamed free ever since.

Seemingly, nearly every comic artist and cartoonist has turned their hand to drawing erotica at some point in their careers, whether through choice or through financial necessity. Carl Barks, Alex Raymond, and even Jack Kirby turned their hand to the odd salacious scribble, although the latter's two-page *Galaxy Green* strip looks positively prudish in comparison with today's comics.

The Eighties, especially, saw an explosion of explicit sequential art in America, thanks in large part to the rise of independent publishers known as the great "black and white explosion." Taking the lead from the counterculture cartoonists, comic stores set out to prove that "comics weren't just for kids." Unfortunately, this invariably involved constant battles with US authorities over censorship, as the federal government failed to realize that the medium had grown and evolved beyond adolescent power-fantasies dressed in brightly colored, skintight, fetishistic outfits.

Erotic comics have always been an important voice for free expression, liberation, and to "cock a snoot" at the establishment. Consequently, they were a key component in the nascent lesbian, gay, bisexual, and transgendered communities, and in the battle for gay rights. Titles like *Gay Comix* and Howard Cruse's strips helped spread a message of tolerance and understanding in a medium that had the most accessibility and direct impact.

But censorship was always around the corner, and when the British Conservative government—under Margaret Thatcher—brought in Clause 28 in 1988, which prevented the "promotion of homosexuality," comic book writer Alan Moore rallied creators to produce the politically motivated *A.A.R.G.H* (*Artists Against Rampant Governmental Homophobia*). It took fifteen years for the act to be repealed.

In 2008 the British government, in a just effort to crack down on pedophiles, proposed outlawing anyone from drawing and creating images of child sex abuse (regardless of context), effectively controlling what people can and cannot create from their imaginations. The viewer is equally as guilty as the artist. This "sledgehammer to crack a walnut" approach is a constant hallmark of poor sexual legislation brought in by various governments over the past one hundred years, legislation that is so wide-reaching it ultimately proves to be unenforceable.

In Japan the seemingly unfettered rise of sexually disturbing manga is coming under increasing international scrutiny, with its apparent pedophilic overtones rightly coming under heavy criticism. The origins of these *hentai* comics and the issues now facing Japanese erotic manga are discussed within, and perhaps serve as a warning sign against completely unregulated comics publishing.

But ultimately, the future of erotic comics is online. Marvel and DC have both launched online comics (for a charge), following the erotic comics before them. Traditional erotic comics publishers have found the increasing Internet demand has eaten into sales of their very graphic novels. Yet the web still suffers from quantity over quality. Included within are some of the better artists and strips that are pushing the medium forward into alternative digital platforms, such as mobile phones.

A word of caution: This book is not for the fainthearted and contains some extremely graphic material, which may shock the less enlightened. How explicit erotic comics have become since the Sixties says a lot. Whereas the Tijuana Bibles are shocking in their frankness, both time and the crudity of the drawings render them somewhat impotent. By contrast, the recent collected albums of erotic sequential art from Europe could almost be acquainted with gynecology textbooks. There's a concern that the old maxim of "less is more" has been thrown out of the window, as implicit has been almost entirely overrun by explicit. This is hardcore.

RISE OF THE COMICS CODE

Comic books have always suffered numerous prejudices that have caused the medium untold damage. Firstly, their name has always implied a humorous edge, an inheritance from the newspapers' "funny pages" that were their progenitor. While humor is perfectly catered for by sequential art, that association in the general public's mind inevitably tars the entire medium with a juvenile brush. It was this perception that comics were only fit for children that saw the entire industry almost destroyed in the mid-1950s, all by the hands of one particularly ardent anti-comic crusader, Dr. Fredric Wertham.

Wertham was an ex-pat German psychiatrist who settled in the United States in 1922. His work examined the effects that environment and social background have on psychological development. After working in several New York psychiatric hospitals, he published his first book, *The Brain as an Organ*, in 1934, and began to focus on the influences of culture and environment on criminal behavior. Dealing with a lot of juvenile criminals who were almost all avid readers of horror and crime comics gave Wertham a view of comics and crime that would prove disastrous for the comic industry.

Wertham first voiced his views in a 1948 article stating that the crime and violence depicted in comics were an important factor in leading kids down the criminal path. But it was the publication of his 1954 book, *Seduction of the Innocent*, which really made an impact. There was already concern about an increasing number of horror comics, like *Tales From The Crypt* and *Vault of Horror*, and Wertham gave readers graphic examples of how comic books depicted sex, crime, murder, sadism, and drugs. *Seduction of the Innocent* caused a sensation, leading to comic burnings and a government investigation.

The witch-hunt was the beginning of the end for a number of publishers, particularly E.C. Comics. Faced with questions from Senator Estes Kefauver and the Senate Subcommittee on Juvenile Delinquency, many frightened comic publishers got together and formed the Comics Magazine Association of America (CMAA). In an effort to save itself from destruction — and rather than face governmental censorship — the CMAA set up a self-regulatory body called the Comics Code Authority (CCA) in October 1954. All comics afterward had to have the seal stating that they were "Approved by the Comics Code Authority" or the majority of newsstands and stores simply wouldn't stock them. Initially, a few refused to join, including E.C. Comics, Dell, and *Classics Illustrated*'s publisher Gilberton.

The CCA set up strict guidelines as to what could and, more importantly, couldn't be represented in their medium. The code prevented the portrayal of everything from "profanity, obscenity, smut, vulgarity, or words or symbols, that have acquired undesirable meanings" to "vampires and vampirism, ghouls, cannibalism, and werewolfism." It even banned using the words "horror" or "terror" in a comic's title.

In terms of sexual content, "Nudity in any form is prohibited, as is indecent or undue exposure," and "Suggestive and salacious illustration or suggestive posture is unacceptable." Erotic comics — or anything even remotely romantic — were effectively neutered, as "Passion or romantic interest" was never to be shown "in such a way as to stimulate the lower and baser emotions." And women were to be drawn as realistically as possible, "without exaggeration of any physical qualities."

Interestingly, even when the code was revised in 1971, the repressive nature was revealed when "seduction" and "rape" were mentioned together in the same sentence, stating that rape shouldn't even be "suggested." The Code's original vagaries were also revealed when it banned "Illicit sex relations," "sexual abnormalities," and "sex perversion" without specifically stating what these actually consisted of. Publishers generally interpreted them as referring to homosexuality.

Ads in comic books were placed under similar restrictions, and the sale of sex instruction books, picture postcards, "pin-ups," "art studies," or any other reproduction of nude or semi-nude figures was prohibited.

Left:
Writer Phil Foglio and artist Matt Howarth's strip from the humorous and erotic independent comic, *XXXenophile* #2. The 1989 comic was the natural offspring of the Sixties' underground comix exploring sexual themes while completely ignoring the Comic Code Authority.

Below and background:
Underground cartoonist Spain Rodriguez's reminiscences in *The Birth of Porn*, which merged the death of E.C. Comics with the rise of *Playboy* magazine. The story appeared in 2003's *Blab!* #14.

DEATH OF THE COMICS CODE

Publishers knew that if they didn't stick to the Comics Code Authority's guidelines and get the literal seal of approval on the cover then it was unlikely that the comic would be distributed, let alone stocked by the numerous dime stores and soda stands that were essential for sales. And so the entire industry knuckled down to creating safe, dry, dull, and unchallenging comics for the next 10–15 years.

Things began to change in the late 1960s when the various Underground Comix artists — inspired by the original E.C. Comics — deliberately started smashing every sexual and social taboo they could find in their own self-published titles. Rather than going through traditional distributors they set up their own networks, reaching thousands who had grown tired of the lifeless superhero fodder offered by the mainstream. Specialist shops, the direct market and the rise of numerous independent publishers in the 1980s meant creators could circumnavigate the old newsstand systems and be free from the CCA's restrictions.

In 1971 the United States Department of Health, Education, and Welfare (today known as the Department of Health and Human Services) asked Marvel Comics editor-in-chief Stan Lee to write a cautionary comic about drug abuse. Lee wrote a three-part *Amazing Spider-Man* story (#96-98), showing drugs as unglamorous and dangerous. Yet the CCA refused to approve the story because it featured narcotics, regardless of the context. "I could understand them," recalled Lee in a 1998 *Comic Book Artist* interview. "They were like lawyers, people who take things literally and technically. The Code mentioned that you mustn't mention drugs and, according to their rules, they were right. So I didn't even get mad at them then. I said 'Screw it' and just took the Code seal off for those three issues. Then we went back to the Code again."

It was the beginning of the end for the code, as its power was obviously out of step with the times. The CCA tried to keep up, repealing its "ban" on homosexuality in 1989, stating that any slur against a character's "sexual preference" should "be clearly shown to be wrong or ignorant." But pretty soon the two largest publishers, Marvel and DC Comics, realized that everyone around them was publishing adult-related material without the Code. In 2001 Marvel opted out of the CCA and used its own age rating system instead. By 2007, only two major publishers, DC Comics and Archie Comics, still submitted certain titles for CCA approval, and the authority had finally lost all credibility, as it failed to keep up with society's fast-changing morality.

History has perhaps treated the man who started it all, Dr Fredric Wertham, unfairly, and he has become a comic book bogeyman. Defending his earlier attacks on comics, he wrote in the 1970s, "My main interest is not in comic books or even mass media, but in children and young people...In the course of that work I came across crime comic books. I had nothing whatever to do directly with the Comics Code. Nor have I ever endorsed it. Nor do I believe in it..." He died at the end of 1981.

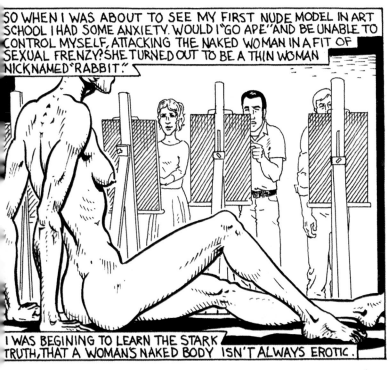

DAVE STEVENS AND BETTIE PAGE IN COMICS

Bettie Page was a legendary pin-up model from the 1950s, who posed for Irving Klaw, the publisher of various erotic fetish photo sets, and comics by artists such as Eric Stanton and Gene Bilbrew. Page's appeal and influence stretched far beyond her modelling years, and she became a cult comic character in the 1980s.

Although he was born in 1955, near the end of Page's modeling career, artist Dave Stevens was drawn toward the retro images of Page in old magazines. The Californian comic creator was so enamored by her look that he used her as a part prototype for a character in his pulp fiction/Republic serial-inspired comic, *The Rocketeer*. Stevens managed to track down Page and asked her permission to use her image in the comic and the two became friends. The strip had an erratic publishing schedule, to say the least, launching in 1982, but not collected until 1988 and 1989 by Comico. The third issue didn't appear for another six years, this time by Dark Horse.

The stormy relationship between the hero, Cliff Secord — The Rocketeer — and his girlfriend Betty was loosely based on Stevens' own on-and-off relationship with actress Charlene Brinkman, AKA "scream queen" Brinke Stevens. Married in 1980 for just six months,

Left:
A beautiful charcoal study by the late, great Dave Stevens reveals his love for retro pin-ups.

Right:
Bettie Page's infamous bondage photos from the 1950s inspired this cartoon study by Jordi Bernet.

Opposite page, right:
This pin-up is a homage to Harvey Comics' cute devil character, Lil' Hot Stuff. Note that Dave Stevens drew the model's breasts realistically, as opposed to the pneumatic beachballs of most female comic characters. The artist also dated the work as 1955, his birth year.

they remained friends and she later modeled for her ex-husband, providing the Bettie Page-esque poses, with Page's face drawn on. Stevens also put in a cameo of his friend, glamour photographer Ken Marcus, as the sleazy "Marco of Hollywood." Since then the artist has drawn numerous Betty pin-up pieces and he became renowned for his 1950s inspired pin-up drawings of women.

In 1987, comic book artist and men's magazine illustrator Greg Theakston started a fanzine, *The Bettie Pages*, which sparked a further interest in Page, and *Playboy* illustrator and erotic artist Olivia De Berardinis has created more than 50 stunning Bettie Page paintings that have been collected into a book. Other artists who were inspired by Bettie Page included Roberto Baldazzini, Steve Woron, Teo Jonelli, and Jim Silke, whose comic debut was 1993's *Rascals in Paradise*, published by Dark Horse Comics. Silke went on to create the popular erotic *Bettie Page* series and Eros Comics also published the tongue-in-cheek *Tor Love Bettie* about a fictional romance between Page and wrestler-turned-Z-movie-actor, Tor Johnson. Page has subsequently appeared on countless comic covers as her beauty and legend live on in never-aging, sequential splendor.

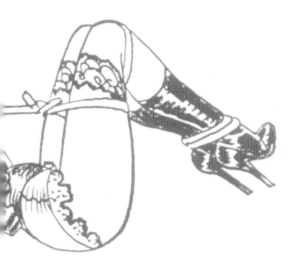

Left:
This 1998 color sketch by Frank Cho has a pencil stroke reminiscent of Spanish erotic artist, Paolo Serpieri. Cho also drew several studies of 1998 Playmate of the Year Tiffany Taylor in a similar style, and the two often did signing events together.

Opposite page:
These unlettered and unpublished strips by Cho express the artist's twin loves of humorous storytelling and erotica.

FRANK CHO

One artist who was inspired by Dave Stevens' delicate line work and pin-up style, and shared a love of Bettie Page, was Frank Cho. Cho was born Duk Hyun Cho in 1971 in Seoul, South Korea. The family moved to the USA when Cho was six, and he soon reveled in Americana. He began drawing comic strips in college and created several strips for the school papers, his most popular being *University*². Like his fellow Korean-American comic artist Jim Lee, Cho studied medicine, and he graduated from the University of Maryland in 1996 with a degree in

Nursing. But rather than pursue a career in health care Cho signed up with Creators Syndicate, Inc., which then syndicated *University*² as *Liberty Meadows*. The strip related the wacky activities of the staff and anthropomorphic "inmates" of the animal sanctuary/rehabilitation clinic. Cho enjoyed huge success with *Liberty Meadows* which mixed crazy humor and sexy women — in the shape of animal psychologist Brandy Carter and her roommate, Jen. Brandy was based on "a composite of several women who I have lusted after since 2nd grade." According to Cho, "She's

based on [*Wonder Woman* actress] Lynda Carter, [fifties pin-up] Bettie Page, [Playboy Playmate] Candy Loving, and two girls from my high school, who, one of them particularly, looked like Brandy."

Brandy's flatmate, Jen, was similarly "...modeled after an old high school acquaintance of mine. She was a hottie," explained the artist on his website. But the series wasn't without its problems. Fed up with being censored by newspaper editors (who objected to the luscious ladies and a chain-smoking Pig called Dean)

Cho decided to self-publish it as a comic book in 2001. The series went on hiatus in 2004, as other projects demanded the artist/writer's attention. In 2007, Cho declared that he was only going to do another 5-6 issues before concluding the series around #44.

Cho has won numerous awards including the Charles Schulz Plaque for Excellence in Cartooning and two Ignatz Awards for Outstanding Artist and Outstanding Comic.

Since *Liberty Meadows* Cho has illustrated other "good girl" series such as *Shanna the She-Devil*, which he also wrote for Marvel Comics, and his similarly themed *Jungle Girl*. Much of Cho's *Shanna* artwork was censored by Marvel when they changed their target audience from 18+ to PG. Cho had revealed a little too much flesh on the "Queen of the jungle" and he was required to cover various flashes of nipples or to draw undergarments on. As fellow comic artist Mike S. Miller noted, "There's a reason *Shanna* went out edited, because Marvel knew they wouldn't make a dime on that book if it went out with the 'creators vision.'"

EROTIC WORLDS OF FRANK THORNE

Frank Thorne started his comic book career in 1948, when he penciled several romance stories at Standard Comics, aged just 18. After graduation, he drew the *Perry Mason* newspaper strip and more comic book work, including *Flash Gordon*, *Jungle Jim*, and *The Green Hornet* for Dell.

As a comic artist in 1950s New York, it's hardly surprising that Thorne came across Irving Klaw. In his graphic memoirs, *Drawing Sexy Women: Autobiographical Sketches*, Thorne recounts his experiences visiting Klaw's "scruffy little shop." Nervous hopefuls stood two-deep, anxious for the opportunity to pore over the thick loose-leaf binders that displayed samples of Irving's colossal inventory of bondage photos," revealed the artist in a frank conversation with Gary Groth in *The Comics Journal* in 2007. Thorne recalled his favorite pin-ups such as Bettie Page, Bunny Pope, and Lynn Davis. "There were offerings other than bondage on Irving's menu. Consider the Junoesque

Irish McCalla — whatta pair she had! He had a binder devoted to strippers: Sherry Britton, Margie Hart, Tempest Storm...I'm beginning to hyperventilate!" joked Thorne. "I was a porn man, still am," he admitted. Yet, despite being such a connoisseur of erotica and the allure of women, Thorne remained a virgin until he was married: "I was whacking the willie so much, I didn't have anything left!"

Thorne was introduced to Klaw via his life model, Bonnie, and attended a photo shoot with her and Bettie Page at the infamous Chelsea Hotel. Thorne described Klaw as a waiter from Smith and Wollensky's, and despite being offered work, Thorne declined. "I was never into bondage, so I backed off working for Irving. I was producing the illustrated history and the pay was better than what Klaw offered. I was getting 25 bucks a pop for the daily feature in the local paper. It ran through 173 issues." Thorne also met Gene Bilbrew in Klaw's office,

jokingly describing him as "the Thomas Kincade of bondage art!"

Thorne's big breakthrough came in 1975, when he was 45, and asked to draw the sexy flame-haired barbarian spin-off from *Conan*, *Red Sonja*, for Marvel. Thorne — along with *Conan* artist Barry Windsor-Smith — was responsible for solidifying the look of the warrior woman in her chain-mail bikini. The artist initially based Sonja on the porn star Lisa De Leeuw and the success of the title helped establish the "erotic fantasy" comics sub-genre. "One of the prouder moments," recalled Thorne, "was when some guy advertised an eight-page *Tijuana Bible* of *Red Sonja* in *The [Comic] Buyer's Guide*. It was called *Red Sonja and Conan, Hot and Dry...* I ordered a dozen!"

He left *Red Sonja* in 1978 to create his own woman warrior, Ghita of Alizzar, the sexy sci-fi series *Lann* for *Heavy Metal* and numerous other stories. He wrote and drew a Lil' Abner pastiche, *Moonshine McJuggs*, for *Playboy* during the 1980s which won him the Playboy Editorial Award for Best Comic, but he later dismissed it as "crude juvenilia."

In the 1990s he created the series *The Iron Devil* and *The Devil's Angel* for Eros Comix, but despite all the erotica, Thorne never went as explicit as his later contemporaries. "That's the dirty little secret of my act. My act is G-rated, but it looks dirty," he said.

THE EROTIC WORLDS OF FRANK THORNE

EROS

FRIG TAMMUZ! PEE ON NEBO AND BAAL! GIVE ME THE DEATH SHAFT!!

Opposite page, left:
Thorne's strip, *The Deathman's Head*, appeared in *The Erotic Worlds of Frank Thorne*. Thorne took his erotic fantasy comics "seriously," to the point of performing stage shows dressed as a wizard, with fellow fantasy artist and *Elf Quest* co-creator, Wendy Pini, dressed as Red Sonja in a tiny metal bikini.

Above:
This version of the cover to the first issue of Eros Comix's *Erotic Worlds of Frank Thorne* (October, 1990) actually appeared inside on page 3, as the cover was censored from showing the naked breasts.

Right:
A panel from *The Deathman's Head* strip, written and drawn by Frank Thorne, which reveals the creator's tongue-in-cheek humor.

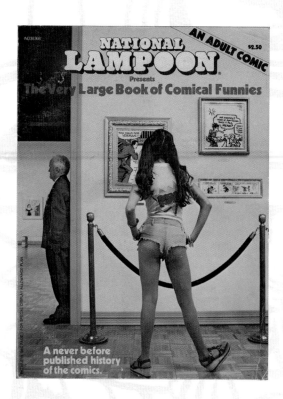

Above:
Cover to National Lampoon's 1975 *Very Large Book of Comical Funnies*.

Opposite page, top left:
A panel from *'Poon*'s "lost" E.C. Comics which featured the work of Walt Simonson, Bernie Wrightson, Russ Heath, Howard Chaykin, and many others.

Opposite page, bottom left:
This underground comix self-parody by S. Clay Wilson and Spain was called *Sap Cosmix* (Zap Comix) and appeared in the *Very Large Book of Comical Funnies*.

Opposite page, right:
This cover to *National Lampoon's Comics* featured luminaries such as Jeff Jones, Vaughn Bodé, and Gahan Wilson.

National Lampoon magazine has a surprisingly long history, dating right back to February 1876 when Harvard University created the humor magazine *Harvard Lampoon*. Almost a century later, this satirical publication went on to sire three Harvard Lampoon alumni, Robert Hoffman, Henry Beard, and Douglas Kenney. When these three decided to launch their own similar magazine in 1970, they enlisted the financial backing of Matty Simmons (co-founder of The Diner's Club and *Weight Watchers Magazine*). The quartet secured the rights from *Harvard Lampoon* to use the name and the first issue of *National Lampoon* was launched in April, 1970. Sex and comics were always at the heart of the magazine, with the first cover featuring a lascivious-looking leather-clad lady and a bizarre cartoon duck with the title "Sexy Cover Issue."

National Lampoon, or *'Poon* as it was affectionately known, always knew its roots were in comic books and the August, 1971 edition had a painting of the court-martialed Vietnam War murderer William Calley parodying *MAD* magazine's mascot Alfred E. Neuman, with the catchphrase, "What, My Lai?," instead of Alfred's "What, Me Worry?"

By 1974 the magazine was selling over a million copies per issue, as many as *MAD* and *Playboy*. The ever-astute Simmons bought out the other three founders that same year for $7.5 million, but many felt this was the beginning of the end of the magazine's "Golden Age."

1974 also saw the magazine take another cue from *MAD* by beginning regular reprints of its material in a series of collections. *National Lampoon Comics*, a collection of the best comic strips from the first four years, included gems such as *Third World Thrills* by P. J. O'Rourke, Dean Latimer, and Gray Morrow, and *Weerd Tayls* by Michel Choquette, Sean Kelly, Joe Orlando, and Frank Springer. Springer

was no stranger to humorous and erotic comics, having previously drawn Phoebe Zeit-Geist for the *Evergreen Review*, which was written by fellow *National Lampoon* contributor Michael O'Donoghue. The writer shone at *National Lampoon*, creating classic comic strips like *Tarzan of the Cows* — in which a baby Lord Greystoke survives a plane crash and is raised by heifers in rural Wisconsin — before heading off to work on *Saturday Night Live*.

In 1975 *'Poon* released *The Very Large Book of Comical Funnies*, which had all new material and was edited by Sean Kelly, and in 1977 the *National Lampoon Presents French Comics (the Kind Men Like)*. Regardless of its poor title, the collection was one of the first to bring European comic erotica to a wider American audience and was one of the foundation stones from which *Heavy Metal* magazine would be built and launched that same year.

Every issue of *'Poon* had a different theme, but the ones that occurred more often than any other were sex and comics. The October, 1976 issue was a "Funny Pages" special with a Superman parody cover. The October, 1978 issue was drawn by Shary Flenniken and the 1984 February "comics special" cover was drawn by fellow female cartoonist Trina Robbins. Many other important cartoonists and illustrators appeared in the magazine's pages and on covers, including Neal Adams, Vaughn Bodé, Edward Gorey, Jeff Jones, Gahan Wilson, and Frank Frazetta.

National Lampoon ultimately spawned many movies, live shows, radio shows, and merchandise, but as these flourished the magazine waned to one edition a year due to underfunding and a lack of new creative talent. Eventually *National Lampoon* magazine ceased publishing with the November 1998 issue, but it lives on as a multimedia company.

HEAVY METAL

In France in the early 1970s many artists were pushing the boundaries of the comic medium, directing it away from the children's traditional humor and adventure stories toward more experimental, darker, and adult material. 1974 saw several creators, including Jean-Pierre Dionnet, Philippe Druillet, Jean Giraud (aka Moebius), and Bernard Farkas founding a new publishing house, Les Humanoïdes Associés. Their cutting-edge adult science fiction/fantasy anthology was *Métal Hurlant* (literally, Screaming Metal), published in December 1974.

Around mid-1975, the *National Lampoon* magazine's team of Editor Tony Hendra and Publisher Leonard Mogel came across some comics which had been bought on a European holiday. *Métal Hurlant* was one of the titles that took this route into the National Lampoon offices. Leonard Mogel liked the style of this magazine so much that he licensed an American version and renamed it *Heavy Metal*.

The first issue of *Heavy Metal* was released in April 1977 and featured mostly translated reprints from the European edition by greats such as Enki Bilal, Jean Giraud, Phillippe Druillet, Milo Manara, Philippe Caza, and the ultra-violent, uber-cool *RanXerox*, by Stefano Tamburini and Tanino Liberatore's. *Heavy Metal*'s blend of dark fantasy/science fiction and erotica was a hit from the start, selling around 144,000 copies per issue. Slowly the magazine swelled its proportion of material from American creators, such as Underground Comix star Richard Corben's epic fantasy *Den*. This lushly painted saga featured full frontal nudity of both sexes, with massively mammaried women and hugely endowed muscle men making out together, like Conan on Viagra.

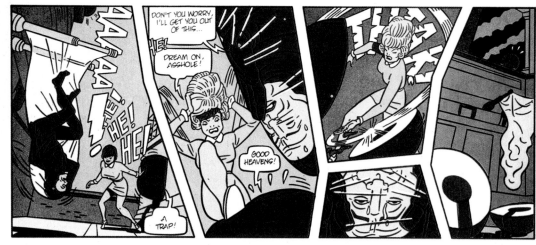

Opposite page, bottom left:
Heroes by Daniel Torres appeared in the July 1990 issue of *Heavy Metal*. It featured a phallic shaped superhero, Super Power, who has two "testicle" sidekicks and is eventually "neutered" by the supervillainess when she captures him in a giant condom. Freud would have been proud.

Opposite page, top right:
Dave Doorman's cover to the January 1994 issue of *Heavy Metal*.

Opposite page, bottom right:
Heavy Metal's May 1992 edition cover was painted by fantasy artist supremo, Julie Bell.

Right:
Alfonso Azpiri's distinctive sexy space epic, *Lorna*, appeared in numerous issues of *Heavy Metal* including this one from July 1990.

Eva Medusa

The founding editors of *Heavy Metal* were Sean Kelly and Valerie Marchant with ex-DC Comics employee John Workman as art director and designer. But by 1979, Leonard Mogel had replaced Kelly and Marchant with Ted White, a highly regarded sci-fi editor who revitalized *Amazing Stories* and *Fantastic* between 1968 and 1978. White and Workman revamped *Heavy Metal*, incorporating more strips by American artists and adding regular columns: Lou Stathis on rock music, Jay Kinney on underground comics, Steve Brown reviewed sci-fi novels, and Bhob Stewart wrote about fantasy films and animation. White's tenure was limited to a year, with Julie Simmons-Lynch taking over as editor in 1980.

The following year saw a feature-length animated movie released, entitled, of course,

Heavy Metal. Produced by Ivan Reitman — with voices by John Candy, Eugene Levy, and others — the film adapted many of the magazine's strips. Made on a budget of around $9.3 million, the film garnered more than $20 million in the cinema. Thanks to the movie's success the magazine's circulation peaked at 234,000 in September, 1982.

In 1986, *Heavy Metal* dropped back to a quarterly schedule, and then went bi-monthly in 1989. After a good 12-and-a-half-year run, Heavy Metal's parent, *Métal Hurlant*, was unfortunately discontinued in July, 1987, its American offspring outliving it.

Simmons-Lynch remained the editor until 1992 when Kevin Eastman acquired the magazine and became both publisher and editor.

Opposite page, top left:
The cover to the steamy Brazilian jungle drama, *Eva Medusa*, written by Antonio Segura and drawn by erotic comic artist Ana Mirallés. The book was published by Heavy Metal/Tundra in English in 1993.

Left:
An erotic moment in *Eva Medusa*, when a young girl's sexual jealously and voodoo powers bring doom upon a plantation household. The book was originally part of a highly charged trilogy first published by Glénat in France in 1991.

Below:
Luis Royo's cover to *Heavy Metal* from January 1995. The Spanish artist also contributed to *National Lampoon* magazine and has a huge fan following for his erotic fantasy paintings. Note the phallic nature of the weapon the woman is holding.

CORBEN! ARTHUR SUYDAM!

JANUARY 1995
$3.95
CAN $4.50

WPS 36587

HEAVY METAL

THE ILLUSTRATED
FANTASY MAGAZINE

®

RETAILER: DISPLAY UNTIL JANUARY 16, 1995

01

7 09093 87 2

Kevin Eastman, co-creator of the slow-burning but eventually huge *Teenage Mutant Ninja Turtles*, acquired *Heavy Metal* for $500,000. "*Heavy Metal* was a really big influence," said Eastman in a *Newsarama* interview in 2007. "I bought the first issue off the newsstands in 1977, around the time I was getting bored with superhero comics and those kinda things. *Heavy Metal* showed me that there was this whole other world of comic book storytelling besides guys running around in tights."

Eastman brought an even more old school "rock and roll" feel to the magazine, full of denim, big bikers, bigger boobs, and — of course — heavy "rawk." The erotic element of the mag was increased with more blatantly salacious stories inside than previously published. *Heavy Metal's* erotic content has surprisingly not gotten it into as much hot water as other similar comic publications. Possibly its magazine format has saved it from the association that it was a comic book, and therefore aimed at kids. However, two issues of *Heavy Metal* did feel the wrath of Canadian customs when the Spring 1988 edition had several pages torn out because of various *Druuna* illustrations by Paolo Serpieri, and the November 1997 issue had one page torn out from *The Gypsy* by Smolderen with art by Enrico Marini.

Eastman produced a second *Heavy Metal* animated feature, *Heavy Metal: F.A.K.K.2*, with a slightly increased budget of $15 million. The straight-to-video 2000 release was based on Eastman and artist Simon Bisley's *The Melting Pot* graphic novel. The central female protagonist was based on glamour model and B-movie actress, Julie Strain, who also happened to be

Right and opposite page, left:
This *Heavy Metal* strip by Simon Bisley highlights the increased erotic elements in the magazine since 1991. Note in the second page, first panel, the artist's self-portrait as a puppet, making a wry comment about working for his friend and publisher, Kevin Eastman, co-creator of *Teenage Mutant Ninja Turtles*.

Eastman's wife. The former *Penthouse* Pet also voiced the character in the movie. But the film failed to achieve the same crossover success of its predecessor.

In July 2002, the French *Métal Hurlant* was resurrected by publishers Les Humanoïdes Associés, for a brief 14-issue run before disappearing again in December 2004.

The US edition of *Heavy Metal* continues to produce quality sci-fi erotica, but its audience has waned somewhat over the decades and it currently sells a modest 60,000 copies per issue.

CHERRY POPTART

Larry Welz was a cartoonist who rode the underground comix wave in the late 1960s, creating his violent and sexually explicit superhero satire strip, *Captain Guts*, in 1969. In 1984 Welz created a one-off parody comic called *Cherry Poptart*. "It was a good idea that I had, but I didn't really have all of the stuff to pull it off," the Fresno-born cartoonist explained on his website. "[I lacked] the right kind of jokes and plots just popping out of my head at regular intervals, the ability to just dash off a proportionally and anatomically correct drawing of a cute sexy naked girl without having to erase it about 50 times and start over." But Welz persisted and it eventually came together.

The strip was a parody of the *Archie* comics and was drawn in a deliberately similar style. Welz's premise was to take the Dan De Carlo-drawn concepts of Riverdale's permanent adolescents and update them for a contemporary readership (something Harvey Kurtzman and Will Elder had previously done in their *Goodman Beaver Goes Playboy* strip in 1962's *Help!*). Whereas Archie, Betty, Veronica, Jughead et. al. would perennially date and hang out at the soda pop stand in a perpetually naive 1950s middle-Americana fantasy, Cherry and her gang would drink booze, take drugs, and — most importantly — fuck, like real teenagers. Needless to say *Cherry* raised the ire of Archie Comics and Welz has been a constant target of controversy dealing with battles over freedom of expression, a potential Kellogg's lawsuit in 1986 demanding the title change to just *Cherry* to avoid confusion over their Pop-Tarts trademark, as if an erotic comic and a breakfast snack are easily mistaken for each other.

Upbeat, naughty, and a little anarchistic, the blonde, sexy, bisexual Cherry is not a passive victim, but is the archetypal sexy "girl next door." The series is, if only on the surface, all about

sex, but at the core is the perennial question, what if sex was always fun, guilt-free, and unaccompanied by fear and violence? *Cherry* is intended as a light-hearted comic, and it exists in a fantasy world where sex has no serious emotional consequences, there is no disease, and nobody ever gets pregnant.

Cherry is eternally horny, as is every character in the series, including her mother, Pepper — a divorced MILF (Mom I'd Like to Fuck) — who often engages in threesomes with Cherry and a boyfriend. Other characters include Johnny Fuckerfaster, Ellie Dee, and the BDSM-loving Lola Palooza (Veronica to Cherry's Betty).

But *Cherry* was always more than just a "fuck book," and it relied heavily on satire and parody, attacking everything from hypocritical morals of politicians and evangelists to parodies of Michael Jackson, *The Wizard of Oz*, *Friday the 13th* movies, *Rambo*, and *Indiana Jones*. Cherry has appeared in several free speech/censorship awareness campaigns and in support of the Comic Book Legal Defense Fund. One comic shop in Florida was busted when it sold the *Cherry Anthology* #1 to an undercover police officer. While the charges were later dropped, this sort of harassment has been the bane of Welz's career, but as Cherry herself says, "Fuck 'em if they can't take a joke! Tee hee!"

Opposite page
Larry Welz's *Cherry* covers always made a joke of social taboos whether it was Satanism or the apocryphal story of sex with gerbils.

Left:
Cherry Poptart's explicit encounter with "The King" who may, or may not, actually be Elvis, in a *Ghostbusters* parody.

OMAHA THE CAT DANCER

Reed Waller created this sexy anthropomorphic "funny animal" series way back in 1978 when he first drew the strip, *The Adventures of Omaha* in the anthology *Vootie*. The character returned in *Bizarre Sex* 9 and 10 (in 1981 and 1982, respectively) and finally got her own series, *Omaha the Cat Dancer*, in 1984. It was first published by SteelDragon Press, before moving to Kitchen Sink Press with issue 3. Kate Worley, Waller's then-girlfriend, started writing the series with issue 2 — helping Waller through his writer's block. The story was a sexually explicit soap, with all the twists, turns, and nuances of a melodrama, and Worley's writing was praised for its confident sex-positive feminist stance. Omaha, the lead character, enjoys her job as a stripper and finds it empowering, rather than degrading, after leaving her sexist office job. She falls in love with Chuck Tabey, but both are pursued by Chuck's mentally ill millionaire father, and former lover of Omaha's.

In 1988, Worley was badly hurt in a car accident and took two years to recover, which slowed the book's frequency. The series created significant controversy with several obscenity charges laid at its door, and both Waller and Worley became active campaigners for cartoonists' First Amendment rights. The Toronto police raided a comic book store, and ludicrously claimed that Omaha, an anthropomorphic comic, depicted bestiality. However, the more progressive New Zealand Indecent Publications Tribunal ruled in 1990 that the series was not indecent as it portrayed sexuality in the context of ongoing emotional relationships in a mature and realistic way.

But tragedy continued to plague the title, when — two years after Worley's crash — Waller contracted colon cancer. Things looked grim until a two-part fund-raising comic, *Images of Omaha*, managed to pay for the artist's medical bills and he made a full recovery. But things were going badly in Waller and Worley's marriage. They divorced, and the comic ceased publication in 1995. The animosity between the two prevented

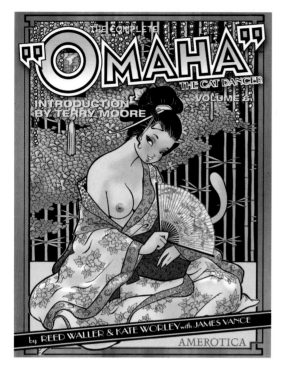

Opposite page, left and right:
Omaha and her lover, Chuck, have a passionate embrace at her workplace. Their dialogue is naturalistic, loving, and a refreshing change from the often silted "porn speak" of modern sex movies.

Above:
NBM's Amerotica edition of *The Complete Omaha the Cat Dancer Volume 6*. Beautifully painted by Reed Waller, it pays homage to Japan's erotic shunga prints.

any more strips for almost a decade. Worley remarried James Vance, a fellow comic scribe and Waller did several personal projects. But cancer stalked the creative pair once more, this time with Worley contracting lung cancer in 2001.

Finally, in early 2004, Waller and Worley managed to reconcile their differences and began working on the final story arc to bring a satisfactory conclusion to *Omaha*. Sadly, Worley wasn't as lucky as her ex-husband and she died on 6 June 2004. Since then Vance and Waller have continued to collaborate on *Omaha*, using Worley's notes, and the series is being serialized in NBM's erotic comic magazine *Sizzle*.

MELODY

While autobiographical comics were not new — with both Justin Green's 1972 *Binky Brown Meets the Holy Virgin Mary* and Robert Crumb's sexual confessions — Sylvie Rancourt and Jacques Boivin's series *Melody* was a departure in terms of the story's ongoing nature. The comic recounted Rancourt's life as an exotic dancer in Canada. Having worked in the Montreal strip clubs for five years she created her comic book alter ego, *Melody*, in 1985.

She soon teamed up with fellow French-Canadian artist Boivin and they produced a one-off comic, *Mélody à Ses Debuts*. In 1988 the Québécois duo went on to produce an ongoing series — *Melody: The True Story of a Nude Dancer* — for one of the original US underground comix publishers, Kitchen Sink. Its initial 10-issue run sold an impressive 120,000 copies in total, and the first four issues were collected into a graphic novel, *The Orgies of Abitibi*. Interestingly, *Melody*'s success ran parallel to that of *Omaha the Cat Dancer*, also published by Kitchen Sink, in 1986 — a deliberate ploy by the publisher to have the two titles compete well together.

Boivin translated Rancourt's scripts as well as drawing them, and went on to write and draw a second series, *Melody On Stage*, for Eros Comix. This dealt with Melody's first audition in a strip club, and the humiliation she went through just to take her clothes off in public.

Montreal's Club Melody, which was open between 1990–1992, even cashed in on the comic's popularity, and Rancourt went on to manage her own Hotel Melody in her native Abitibi, Northern Quebec, with its own strip bar.

Ironically, Rancourt and Boivin's comics are hard to find in their home country, thanks to notoriously over-zealous vice squads and Canadian customs' border censorship. The comic book stores have, for the most part, acquiesced silently, with only a few voices of dissent, such as Boivin, trying to make a difference.

THE TRUE STORY OF A NUDE DANCER

No. 8
ULTS ONLY

Melody ™

$2.50
($3.00 Canada)

Okay
BEC

by
Sylvie
Rancourt
with
Jacques
Boivin
and
Gabriel
Morrissette

No. 6
ADULTS ONLY
$2.00
$2.40 Canada

Melody

CHE

by Sylvie Rancourt with Jacques Boivin and Gabriel Morrissette

Opposite page, bottom:
Interior pages from *Melody*, where a character explains how they developed their fetish for being spanked.

Left:
The cover to *Melody* #8 drawn by Jacques Boivin and subtitled "The true story of a nude dancer."

Above:
Less is more on this cover to *Melody* #6, which asks many questions of the reader.

SQP

Describing themselves as "your one-stop source for the very finest in friendly female eye-candy!" two self-professed Brooklyn fanboys — Sal Quartuccio and Bob Keenan — set up Sal Quartuccio Publishing (SQP) in 1973. Starting out with an appreciation for fantasy and comic art, they turned their passion into a substantial business with a global customer base.

They published limited-edition portfolios, magazines, and graphic novels, showcasing new artists from around the world, "All blessed with a talent for illustrating the female form in all its curvy delights!" Despite having been in the industry for 35 years, "We still get people at conventions looking at us like we just dropped off the mothership," noted Quartuccio and Keenan, bemused.

While the majority of their output consists of pin-up books and collections of erotic imagery, paintings, and illustrations, SQP have produced numerous sexy sequential stories such as Enrique Villagran's *Teach Me!* and *Teach Me Too!* which tell the "highly charged story of sexual chemistry" between three female teachers "set to explode in a climax of mutual delight!"

Right:
Blas Gallego's *Sex Throughout the Ages: The Middle Ages* is reminiscent of the work of *O Wicked Wanda* artist, Ron Embleton. The caption reads, "What to do on those long, steamy Knights!"

Opposite page, top right:
A humorous strip, *A Friend in Need*, from Blas Gallego's *The Very Breast of Dolly* collection, published by SQP in 2005. The character owes much to Harvey Kurtzman and Will Elder's *Little Annie Fanny*, both in looks and storytelling.

Opposite page, bottom right:
Dolly's Creatures of the Night, also by erotic fantasy artist Gallego.

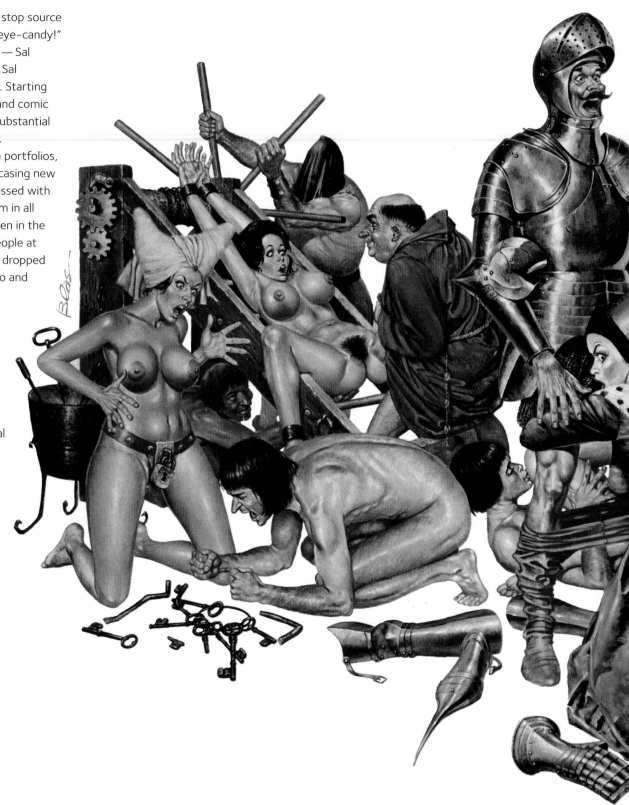

RICH LARSON AND STEVE FASTNER

Another SQP graphic novel was *Demon Baby: Hell on Heels* by two of the publisher's most popular and prolific creators, Steve Fastner and Rich Larson. The creative duo have worked with the publisher since the late-1970s, and were introduced to each other in the mid-1970s by comics fan and writer Larry Becker at a Minneapolis comic convention. Admirers of each other's art, they teamed up to work on several paintings and sold their first published piece to SQP for the cover of the publisher's sci-fi and fantasy comic anthology *Hot Stuf'* #6, starting a relationship that would last more than 30 years.

"In the '80s," recalled Fastner, "Sal hired us to do Marvel superhero portfolios." But as Larson pointed out, "We're pretty under-the-radar as far as comics fans are concerned. Later on, we started illustrating SQP fantasy female portfolios and art books, and still do." The pair work by Larson coming up with an idea and creating a tight pencil drawing. Fastner scans the drawing into Photoshop, and prints out a clean, light copy on bond paper. He then paints over the copy with markers and airbrush acrylic paints.

Fastner's artistic admiration extended towards classic fantasy and erotic artists like Richard Corben, Frank Frazetta, and Wally Wood, among others. Larson was inspired by "the more innocent pin-up art styles of the '50s and '60s. I spent a lot of my wayward youth rummaging around in the basements of used bookstores for old comics, and I'd invariably come across boxes of old men's magazines, spicy pulps, and paperbacks with lurid covers," the artist recalled. "All of this burned itself into my impressionable, not very large brain, and to this day, I can't resist working it into our own art."

CONTROVERSY: BARRY BLAIR

Barry Blair was born in Ottawa, Canada, and was adopted by a Taiwanese couple when he was 9. The new family moved to Taiwan and this became an important influence in his work, with the artist even adopting the pseudonym Bao Lin Hum for a while. "I did a lot of learning and looked at Chinese artwork and things," he said. Blair was a self-taught creator, and by 1980, in his mid-teens, he began self-publishing his fantasy epic *Elflord*. Blair was heavily influenced by another fantasy comic, *ElfQuest*, by Richard and Wendy Pini, as well as by erotic comics pioneer Wally Wood.

Blair co-founded his own imprint, Aircel Comics, and produced numerous fantasy titles, but when the company fell into financial difficulties the creator sought the help of fellow publisher, Malibu. "... [The] reason I did this was because I wanted to keep my guys [at Aircel] employed. Part of the deal was they would continue doing their books. However, all of a sudden Malibu started saying: 'Well, I think you ought to do these adult books...'" With massive debts to pay off Blair chose to draw erotic comics rather than declare bankruptcy. Series like *Leather & Lace* (1989), *Climaxxx* (1991) *Sapphire and Vampyre's Kiss* (1990) sold very well and Blair soon found himself cornered by his own success. "My first concern was: 'What's this going to do to my career?' I want to be known as the guy who does these adventure books, and very soon I got to be known as the guy who does the sex books... [However] I had a lot of fun doing the really goofy stories in *Leather & Lace*..." *Leather & Lace* and *Sapphire* were essentially X-rated versions of *Elflord* and *Samurai*, but Blair was allegedly becoming increasingly uncomfortable. Eventually he phoned Malibu and told them he couldn't draw erotic titles anymore, "I was 70% of their income and they just panicked. They just lost their minds! They were gonna come and kill me or

whatever. 'You know you can't stop!' And I just said: 'Forget it. I want to go back and do *Samurai* and *Elflord*.' And they said: 'Well, do them as SEX books!' So I add: 'Look. I'll give you Aircel. You can have it. You've never paid for it or anything. But you can use it and put all your porno crap into it and just go nuts.'"

Blair has often been at the forefront of controversy regarding the sexual content of his comics, receiving criticism over the apparent under-age appearance of near-naked, sexually ambiguous, intertwined characters. His comics lost direction and became long black and white panoramas of pubescent boys being stripped, bound, and tortured.

In a 1995 interview with *Podium*, Blair denounced all his early '90s work and that of erotic comics in general. "I really hate the idea that the whole comic industry is turning into this weird sort of...it's not even a smut factory. It's not even that good. If they just published real vile pornography, at least they would have accomplished something...It's just this weird sort of soft porn titillation stuff," bemoaned Blair. "I guess the people doing it don't really know where they're going with it, you know? I mean you've got women with huge breasts sort of having these pseudo-lesbian relationships on this imaginary Paradise Island thing..."

Blair moved to Europe and worked there for several years, inspired by European illustrators such as Pierre Joubert. But the Canadian artist eventually returned to the sub-genre that made him infamous, erotic fantasy comics, with two new *Sapphire* albums for NBM in 2001-2002 and a three-part story in the publisher's erotic anthology *Sizzle*. In 2005, Blair and his partner, Colin Chan (aka Colin Walbridge), created *Nymphettes: The Erotic Elvish Art of Barry Blair and Colin Walbridge*, for SQP, with pin-ups of various semi-clad female Elves.

Opposite page, top right:
A recent study of an erotic elf by Blair.

Opposite page, bottom right:
A pin-up by Blair and Colin Walbridge.

Left:
A page from Barry Blair's *Climaxxx* #1. Blair plays with traditional superhero conventions when a scientist persuades Kiki that his "super serum" will turn her into a super heroine, in an erotic echo of Captain America's origin.

Below:
The cover to *Climaxxx* #1 published by Aircel in 1991.

CONTROVERSY: FAUST

Another series that managed to polarize comic book readers and critics was writer David Quinn's and artist Tim Vigil's *Faust*. The series was a loose interpretation of the Dr. Faustus legend, set in contemporary New York. John Jaspers is a mental patient who becomes the lover of his female psychiatrist, Jade de Camp. After disappearing from the asylum, Jaspers sells his soul to the devil, disguised as a criminal mastermind known as M (aka Mephistopheles). Jaspers is, in true comic book style, transformed into a costumed, near-invulnerable vigilante, armed with deadly metal claws, looking like a cross between Batman and Wolverine. Jaspers becomes too unstable to control and the costumed maniac starts preying upon the underworld that M partly controls. "...there is a supernatural basis to the idea of demons and the devil and [Faust] and the comic. So it's not totally, totally natural," explained co-creator and artist Tim Vigil.

The series contained strong graphic violence and explicit sexual situations, often combined in over-the-top excessiveness previously only seen in the underground comics of S. Clay Wilson. Apart from the excessive sex and Quinn's intelligent writing, it was Vigil's heavily detailed, and anatomically precise artwork that made the series stand out. The first series: *Faust: Love of the Damned* was published in 1989, but suffered from erratic publishing schedules. However this didn't prevent cult director Brian Yuzna from disastrously adapting it for the big screen in 2001. The second series, *Faust: Book of M*, was nominated for the 1999 Bram Stoker Award for Best Illustrated Narrative.

The series was almost certainly an inspiration for Todd McFarlane's slightly more kid-friendly phenomena, *Spawn*, with similar themes of a tortured, costumed vigilante whose soul is tied to Hell.

Quinn went on to write *Dr Strange* for Marvel Comics and Vigil, having been an originator of the genre, carried on drawing dark horror/sex comics, working at Glenn Danzig's Verotik Publishing on *Dark Horror of Morella*, as well as working toward the final ending for *Faust*.

Opposite page, far left:
Panels from *Faust*'s 1998 sequel, pencilled by Tim Vigil and "embellished" by Johnny B. Stylistically, *Faust* appealed to hard rock and metal fans, with its depiction of extreme sex and tattooed characters.

Opposite page, bottom:
The variant covers to *Faust 777: The Wrath* #3 and #1, published by Avatar Press, and *Faust* #11 of the original series. *The Wrath* #0 had no less than eight variant covers.

Above:
Explicit language and graphic imagery caused outrage for many retailers when *Faust* first appeared. This page is from #11 of the original *Love of the Damned* series.

Right:
A page from the original 1989 *Faust* series by Tim Vigil.

BLACK KISS

Howard Chaykin is no stranger to controversy and erotica, having made his breakthrough in comics in late 1970s, drawing *Cody Starbuck*, *Ironwolf Star Wars*, and *Dominic Fortune*. His star continued its ascent when he wrote and drew his political adult sci-fi series *American Flagg* in 1983. *Flagg* featured pre- and post-coital scenes but was always tastefully done.

But when Chaykin released *Black Kiss* — through the now-defunct Canadian publisher, Vortex, in 1988 — all hell broke loose. *Black Kiss* was a hardboiled erotic story set in the sleazy world of '80s L.A. which owed a nod, in tone at least, to the novels of James Ellroy.

The 12-issue miniseries told the story of Cass Pollack, a deadbeat jazz musician and ex-heroin addict who is on the run from the police and the Mafia after the latter kill his family. Dagmar Laine, a prostitute and lover to 1950s movie star Beverly Grove, are both searching for a reel of film taken from the Vatican's collection of pornography. Laine and Grove hire Pollack to steal the reel in return for them providing him with an alibi to square things with the police.

Chaykin's story was typically full of convoluted plot twists and turns, and none more surprising than when one of the central protagonists, Dagmar, turns out to be a pre-operative transsexual vampire.

Black Kiss quickly became one of the most controversial US comics of the late 1980s thanks to Chaykin's unflinching portrayal of explicit sex and violence previously unseen in "mainstream" comics at that period. To help retailers prevent possible litigation in comic shops (which were generally perceived as kiddie stores) Vortex shipped copies of *Black Kiss* in pre-sealed plastic bags. This meant that casual browsers could not open the comic and see the internal content.

Describing *Black Kiss*, fellow comics scribe Matt Fraction wrote, "In terms of sex, this is Chaykin rejecting the 'mature comics' movement of the '80s by exploiting all of the totemic sex fetishes the comics world had loved him for to

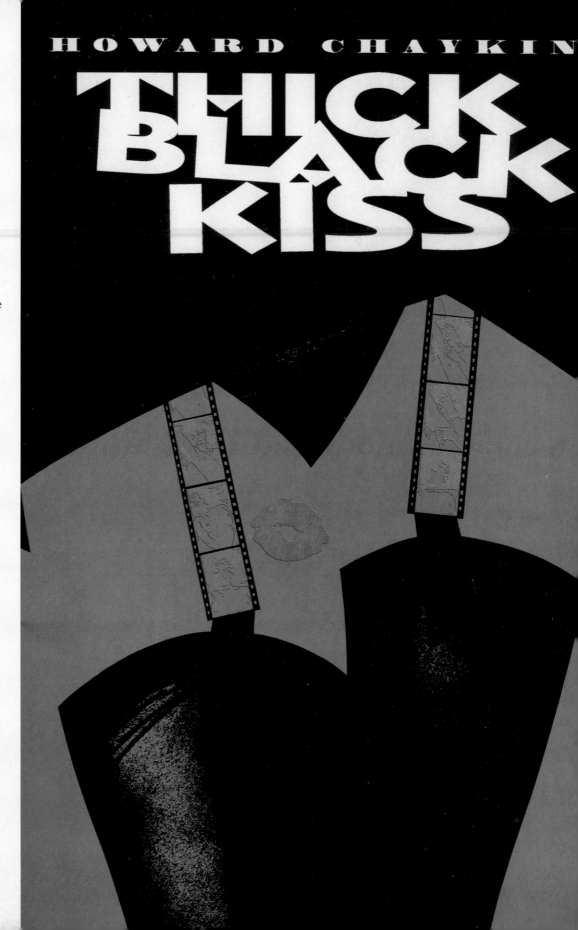

Left:
Chaykin's series featured just about every single conceivable sex scenario, with incredibly verbose participants.

Above and opposite page, left:
Pollack infiltrates the secret sex cult in *Black Kiss*. Chaykin's page layout and design skills—which he'd honed previously on *American Flagg*—are exhibited here in the way he integrates the banner headline text and panel construction.

Opposite page, bottom right:
The cover to *Black Kiss* #9 (in 1988).

date: big asses and hiked-up skirts; garters and blow jobs...The final irony of *Black Kiss* is that Chaykin holds his subject matter, medium, and (one presumes) his audience in such contempt that he won't even let them enjoy the fucking in this, his dirty little fuck book..."

"I think *Black Kiss* is one of the funniest things I've ever done, a darkly funny comedy," recalled Chaykin in a *Newsarama* interview almost 20 years after the first issue came out. "I did it at a turning point in my life. I turned the point and now I'm done." Chaykin has been pitching for the comic to be adapted into a movie: "There's no reason that film couldn't be made. I don't think it would be a PG-13, but it could be done anywhere from a hard R to an X...And there have been a number of situations where it was almost there. We've had a number of almosts, in the first place with a semi-well-known Canadian actress, another time with a very well-known American director. Hollywood is filled with almosts. I'm still hoping someday to get it happening. That's one of the reasons that I like that it remains in print."

Vortex collected the series into volumes called *Big Black Kiss* in 1989. The series has been collected into paperback format several times as *Thick Black Kiss*, the most recent being in 2000 with an edition released by Eros Comix.

Black Kiss paved the way for other creators to brave the genre. "I'm really tired of reading sex stuff by guys who have never had a date," bemoaned Chaykin unfairly a few years later, referring to the glut of erotic comics that followed *Black Kiss*' success. "I mean, it was bad enough reading mad scientists by guys who had never gotten out of high school, but now that we're writing sex it's even worse!"

Black Kiss was, and remains, an important erotic comic as it was one of the first to cross over from the murky subgenre into the mainstream thanks to its high profile creator. It broke taboos and new ground and forced the US comic book industry to reassess what the Europeans had discovered 20 years earlier — namely that comics could deal with sexual issues for an adult readership, and that a mature public would buy them.

EROS AND THE FBI

Thanks to the rise of the do-it-yourself ethos of the underground comix movement of the 1960s, and the repressive nature of the Comics Code Authority, many new creators, distributors, and retailers started to circumnavigate the old systems of getting comics to an eager public. As specialist comic shops started to flourish in America, so did independent publishers and fanzines. One such company, Fantagraphics Books, Inc. (aka FBI), was founded earlier than most, in 1976, by Gary Groth and Mike Catron, and was directly inspired by the underground comix and work by Robert Crumb, S. Clay Wilson, and the like. The following year, Kim Thompson joined the company and became a co-owner with Groth. Initially formed to publish the critical trade magazine *The Comics Journal*, the company branched out into publishing comics in 1982 with Gilbert and Jaime Hernandez's *Love & Rockets*. They went on to publish and support many ground-breaking creators such as Peter Bagge, Dan Clowes, Joe Sacco, Chris Ware, and Jessica Abel. Fantagraphics soon established a reputation for publishing innovative titles that traditional comics companies (such as Marvel and DC) either didn't know existed or wouldn't touch, including serious, dramatic, historical, journalistic, political, and unsurprisingly, sexual themes. As *The Village Voice* noted, "It'd be difficult to find more challenging and entertaining rabble-rousers amid the panorama of popular culture."

Right:
Ron Wilber's 1990 three issue miniseries, *Domino Lady*, was an erotic homage to the "spicy" pulp novels of the 1930s and 40s, and to the character herself, who first appeared in 1936's *Saucy Romantic Adventures*.

NUMBER 1 OF 3 $1.95 IN THE U.S. ($2.25 IN CAN.)
ADULTS ONLY

DOMINO LADY

A New Series
REVELRY IN H
Ron Wilber

© WILBER 90

EROS comix

PLEASURE,
ISS PATRICK.

DELGLYN, WE'VE
GOT PROBLEMS.

WHAT'S
HAPPENING?

But lofty ideals of promoting comics as art didn't pay the bills and Fantagraphics hit financial problems in the late '80s. Needing to make money quickly, Groth and Thompson turned to a sure-fire seller—sex—and launched *Eros Comix* in 1990. "Porn came to us in a vision," joked Thompson. Many saw the new imprint at odds with *The Comic Journal's* high ideals, but Groth remained unrepentant: "The criticism doesn't discomfort me in the least. The only criticism that bothers you is criticism that's on target. The porn we publish is invoked by perennial carpers as the last, sputtering criticism when they can't make anything else stick. Publishing porn to subsidize literary work is practically a tradition in lit publishing, so my impurity doesn't bother me much." When pushed, in an interview by *Sequential Tart* in 2000, about Fantagraphics lack of superhero comics, yet its willingness to cash in with the Eros line, Groth simply replied, "I like sex. I don't like superheroes."

Left:
A page from *Domino Lady* #1, subtitled, *Hell's Fanged Horror of Doom!* Domino, AKA Ellen Patrick, became a crime fighter to avenge the death of her district attorney-father.

Below:
Ron Wilber created a sequel to the original series, *Domino Lady's Jungle Adventure*.

WIT "DA DOC IN 'DA DRIVERS SEAT WE LIVED LIKE KINGS. 'DA NATIVES COULDN'T RESIST 'DAT FLUTE.

Eros' initial line-up was an eclectic mixed bag of titles, including *The Erotic Worlds of Frank Thorne*, *I Wanna Be Your Dog* by Ho Che Anderson, *Wendy Whitebread, Undercover Slut* by Don Simpson, *Liaison Delicieuses* by Richard Forg, and *Birdland* by Gilbert Hernandez. The latter was described as a "voyeuristic foray into the lives of several strippers, bodybuilders, horny aliens, and a sensuous psychiatrist" and was typical of Eros' original plan of publishing intelligent erotica, both originated by US creators and European reprints. Sex sells, and *Eros Comix* sold very well, bankrolling Fantagraphics for several years.

Eros' quality has varied greatly over the years, but has always known its origins, publishing *Tijuana Bibles*, classic work by Eric Stanton, and Kate Worley's and Reed Waller's *Omaha the Cat Dancer*. Sadly, the titles of many comics didn't stand up to scrutiny, such as *Tales from the Clit* and *Aunts in your Pants* by Enrico Teodorani and *The Sexual Misadventures of Kung Fu Girl* by Kono Yaro, which suggested a cheesy porn movie ethic, rather than sophisticated erotica.

Left:
Dinosaur porn from *Birdland* indicates that creator Gilbert Hernandez perhaps wasn't taking his erotica series entirely seriously.

Opposite page:
Gilbert Hernandez initially came to fame via his women-positive strips in *Love & Rockets*, which had a huge female following. So when he created the hardcore erotic miniseries, *Birdland*, for Eros Comix, many of his fans were surprised, shocked, and dismayed, despite several characters from *L&R* appearing in it.

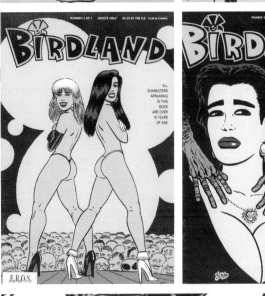

Throughout the 1990s Eros was one of the highest profile and most important publishers of erotic comic books, paving the way for many other publishers to enter the genre. There is no area of sexual fetishism that Eros hasn't published, from hardcore BDSM to sexual parodies of *Buffy the Vampire Slayer* and *The X-Files*. Comedy is an important part of many titles, as Eros is acutely aware of the ridiculousness of human beings in the pursuit of sexual gratification.

These days Eros Comix has diversified into being a retailer of other publishers' erotica (such as NBM) and of DVDs and Japanese erotic manga, known as Hentai. Eros' catalog has over 470 items in it, mostly adult comic books, yet Fantagraphics is less dependant on the erotic imprint now, as the rest of the planet has finally caught up with the parent company's worldview of comics as art. This, combined with the rise of erotic comics on the Internet, has meant that Eros, while publishing important and intelligent work, potentially faces challenges in the future.

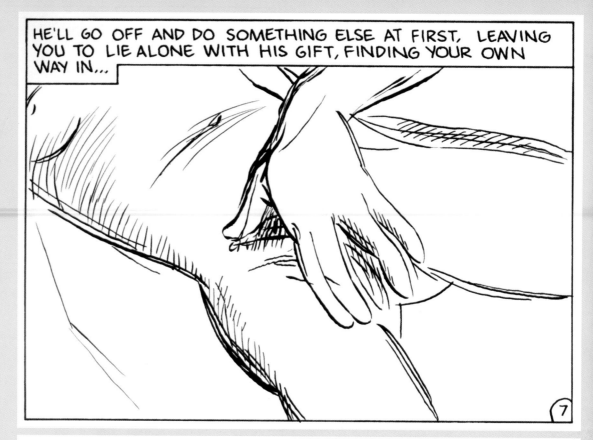

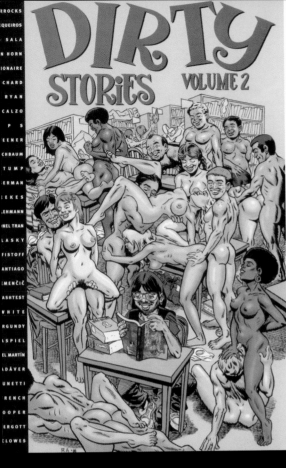

Opposite page:
Panels from New Zealander Dylan Horrocks'
uninhibited—and tender—story, *The First Time*,
from Eros Comix's second volume of the erotic
anthology, *Dirty Stories*.

Above:
The orgiastic cover to 2000's *Dirty Comics #2*
by Rick Altergott.

Right:
This *Spider-Man* parody, *One Thousand Pardons*
by David Lasky and "Many Hands," featured
Peter (AKA Skeeter-Man) having to cope with
inadvertently acquiring an 83-foot long penis.

ALTERNATIVE COMICS, ALTERNATIVE SEX?

But while Eros' erotic comics have become increasingly threatened by the internet, Fantagraphics has grown in popularity with a more general audience, and went on to introduce adult themes into their "mainstream" titles. The main difference with these titles was their approach to sex was never solely to titillate or arouse the readers but, rather, to incorporate sex into stories as a fact of everyday life, and to examine themes related — but not wholly dedicated — to sex.

A good example of how sex was importantly — yet non-sensationally — covered in Fantagraphics' titles was *Love & Rockets*. Both creators, Jaime (Xaime) and Gilbert (Beto) Hernandez, wrote and drew sexual situations sensitively and empathically. Jaime's strip, initially called *Mechanics*, had a maturing and well fleshed out cast, which dealt with the on-again/ off-again love affair between two girls, Maggie and Hopey, living in a tough barrio known as Hoppers. But Jaime's presentation of the affair wasn't a sleazy fanboy drool-fest of hot lesbian girl-on-girl action, despite sex scenes appearing. In fact, Jaime's portrayal of the romance was so favorable that in the late-Eighties they became positive role models for the increasingly vocal lesbian movement.

Another example of how the mature "alternative" scene treated sex was Charles Burns' *Black Hole*. Originally serialised as a 12-issue miniseries from Kitchen Sink and Fantagraphics, it was collected into a graphic novel by Michael Joseph/Pantheon in 2005. The Harvey Award–winning story continued themes Burns had been exploring in the anthology *RAW* with his *Big Baby* and *Skin Deep* series, that of paranoia, puberty, sexual insecurities, alienation, and sexually transmitted diseases.

Inspired by Burns' own school days, the tale is set in suburban Washington state in the mid-1970s, Black Hole focuses on a group of high school students who hang out smoking pot and trying to get laid. However, there's a

weird disease, "the bug," going around that when contracted through intercourse starts to mutate the students in various ways. The story touches on themes explored by film director David Cronenberg, and while there are certainly arousing erotic moments between the central characters Keith and his soon-to-be-girlfriend Chris, the overall effect of the story is more likely to pour cold water on any young man's ardour than to help him rise to the occasion.

Another implicit story of sexual awakening was the much less creepy *Blankets* by Craig Thompson. Thompson's semi-autobiographical 600-page magnum opus stemmed from a simple idea: to describe what it feels like to sleep next to someone for the first time. Coming from a deeply Christian family Thompson didn't believe in sex before marriage, and so we see his romance and sexual explorations, without he and his girlfriend breaking their chastity vows. The book portrays sex as a deeply tender sharing of two people with each other, and remains a positive approach to sex in sequential art.

These, and many more titles, made creators realize that they could discuss sexual

experiences — either their own, in Joe Matt and Julie Doucet's case, or as crass slapstick in Johnny Ryan and Ivan Brunetti's — with the freedom and intelligence their underground progenitors had done 20 years previously. Certainly Matt's masturbatory confessions in *Peepshow* owe everything to Robert Crumb's pioneering work.

Above:
The gorgeous and irrepressible Penny Century (aka Beatríz García) from *Love and Rockets*. Here Jaime Hernandez pays homage to classic cheesecake pin-up artists of the 1950s, particularly in the first panel.

Opposite page, left:
Charles Burns' black and white brushstrokes on *Black Hole* give the story a David Lynch dream-like quality of eroticism mixed with unease and disquiet.

Opposite page, top right:
Hopey goes down on Maggie in a car, in a rare color strip by Jaime Hernandez, from the *Locas in Love* graphic novel.

Opposite page, bottom right:
Thompson and then-girlfriend, Raina, explore the limits of their sexuality in the award-winning *Blankets*, published by Top Shelf in 2003.

NBM

Launched in 1976 by publisher Terry Nantier while still at University, NBM was originally called Flying Buttress Publications. Inspired by his teen years in Paris where he first encountered bande dessinées (French comics and "albums"), Nantier formed a partnership with Chris Beall and Marc Minoustchine, and the company changed its name to NBM, using their last initials for the new title. Like Gary Groth at Fantagraphics, Nantier recalled he "was not interested in publishing superheroes, but reaching as wide a potential audience as possible. In those days, there were no independent comics...the only thing close [were] undergrounds."

Above:
Extreme hardcore comics in Frans Mensink's *Kristina, Queen of Vampires*, published by NBM in 2005.

Right:
Banana Games by Christian Zanier was published by NBM in America and Tabou in France. This high-octane sex 'n' violence version of *Thelma and Louise* (where one is a pre-op transsexual) was very successful.

Opposite page:
The *Queen of Vampires*, staked through the heart and buried, only to rise 200 years later when a criminal is murdered above her grave and his blood revives her. The series mixes cop drama, supernatural elements, and sex scenes.

Racket Ramba, a MAD-like detective story spoof by French artist Loro was NBM's first imported title in the spring of 1977, around the same time as *Heavy Metal* first appeared. "In the first few years, it was very tough going," Nantier recalled. "The concept was pretty radical at the time."

While similarly inspired by the quality of material being produced in Europe — just as *Heavy Metal* was — NBM took a slightly different route to publishing it in the United States. It was one of the first publishers to bring the concept of the graphic novel, or album as they are called in France, to America. It launched with such legendary creators as Enki Bilal and Hugo Pratt, and erotic comic artists Milo Manara and Georges Pichard.

In the early '90s NBM moved into the erotic publishing area substantially when it launched its two imprints *Eurotica* and *Amerotica*, featuring the best sex comics from both continents, ensuring the work was "something that pushes the envelope, even if in a small way, something fun to read and not empty headed." One of their earliest titles was a translation of *The Illustrated Kama Sutra* by Georges Pichard in 1991.

Eight years later, both imprints were going so well that in 1999 NBM's *Eurotica* launched the ground-breaking erotic comic anthology, *Sizzle*. The first issue featured the typical mixture of US and European creators, with strips including *Live Nude Girl* by Petra Waldron and Jennifer Finch, *Shadow and Light — The Arrangement* by Quinn, *Grin and Bare it* by Dany (Daniel Henrotin), and *Emily's Secret* by Marcus Gray.

The anthology has gone from strength to strength, with its quality of writing and art improving with every issue. It has picked up many leading lights in erotic comics including bondage artist Michael Manning (who also had one of his first Graphic Novels — *The Spider Garden* — published by *Amerotica* in 1991), and published all new adventures of *Omaha the Cat Dancer* by Reed Waller, James Vance, and Kate Worley.

NBM still support their mainstream material with more cutting edge and explicit works in the erotic comic genre, and the company has grown to become the second largest indie comics publisher after Fantagraphics, with a $3 million annual turnover and over 200,000 graphic novels sold a year. It continues to produce excellent erotica and, in its own words, "Comics that are shameless, not shameful!"

Left:
Michael Manning and Patrick Conlon's sexy science fiction series, *Tranceptor*, appeared in *Sizzle* magazine before being collected in two volumes to date, the first being *Tranceptor: The Way Station* in 1998.

Left:
Several panels from Colin Murray's strip *The Palace of a Thousand Pleasures*, starring Vikki Belle. This story was Vikki's third saucy romp which had a cheeky humor akin to Britain's *Carry On…* movie series.

Above:
More no-holds-barred pages from Manning and Patrick Colon's sexy science fiction series, *Tranceptor*.

Right:
The cover to NBM's erotic anthology magazine, *Sizzle* #34, with art by Manning and Conlon. This actually became the cover to *Tranceptor: Book Two: Iron Gauge (Part One)* published in 2007.

The End

VEROTIK: DEATH METAL AND DAMES

Glenn Danzig — the hard rock/punk musician, and singer/songwriter for legendary bands such as The Misfits, Samhain, and Danzig — was always a comic book fan and collector, and originally wanted to write and draw comics, but music got in the way.

However, he carried on collecting comic art. "He bought several of my originals once his career had blossomed," recalled comic maestro Mike Kaluta, who went on to paint the cover for Danzig's *Black Aria* album. Danzig's sense of the dramatic stood him in good stead, as did his love of horror and gore. After a successful and long musical career, encompassing horror punk rock, heavy metal, and industrial, to blues and classical, and having influenced Metallica, Rob Zombie, and Guns N' Roses, Danzig returned to his first love, comics, when he set up his own publishing company, Verotik, in the early 1990s.

The company concentrated on mature-themed comics featuring demonic babes who were sexy to look at but would tear your heart out, quite literally. Danzig was initially inspired by artists like fantasy legend Frank Frazetta, comics king Jack Kirby, and '70s underground comix, but Verotik's titles also appealed to *Heavy Metal* and *Faust* readers, and Danzig's hard rock fans.

Danzig sought out artists who had a similar "rawk" (rock music) edge about them and could draw sexy women with attitude. He became friends with *2000 AD* and *Heavy Metal* artist Simon Bisley, who also played drums in his own rock band in the UK. For over 15 years Bisley has drawn plenty of buxom beauties for Verotik, as well as more esoteric projects, such as an adaptation of Milton's *Paradise Lost*.

Another hardcore artist who joined the Verotik stable was Martin Emond, a New Zealand cartoonist and painter. In the early stages of his career he illustrated *White Trash*, a satirical journey through the USA featuring parodies of Elvis and Guns N' Roses lead singer, Axl Rose.

Emond designed several sexy covers for Glenn Danzig's Verotik line, album covers for Evilive Records, and his rock chick illustrations were used as screenprints for the streetwear label Illicit. But Emond was a troubled soul—battling with severe depression—and he committed suicide in L.A. in March, 2004.

As his friends recalled at his funeral, Emond lived the rock'n'roll lifestyle: "He was snakeskin cowboy boots, he was rock'n'roll, he was Enter The Dragon, he was 'Throw up your motherfuckin goats', he was T.N.T, he was dy-na-mite…"

Most of Verotik's characters, such as Satanika and Verotika, exist in a cohesive universe — Verotik World — and often crossed-over into each others' titles, just as Marvel and DC characters did. Verotik's impressive roster of comics included *Akuma She*, *Albino Spider of Dajette*, *Dark Horror of Morella* (featuring art by *Faust* co-creator Tim Vigil), *Devilman*, *G.O.T.H.*, *Igrat*, *Inquisitor Jaguar God*, *Sunglasses After Dark*, *Venus Domina*, and *Wing*Bird*.

In recent years there has been a trend for movie adaptations of Verotik's more salacious titles, notably Ed Lee's *Headers* and *Grub Girl*. The latter, directed by Craven Moorehead, featured porn star Brittney Skye as a zombie hooker, looking for vengeance. The tongue-in-cheek horror/porn flick is described as "sucking dick and chomping guts never looked so good!" Danzig himself moved into producing and directing movies and adapted one of his Verotik titles, *Ge Rouge*, for the big screen as well as his short story, *She Only Likes Men*, from *Verotika* #9.

The modern-day renaissance man has been constantly aware of pushing the comics medium. "If an adult's comics purchases are still limited to *Superman* and *The X-Men*, I think he or she needs their head examined," said the comic publisher/writer. "There's nothing wrong with those titles, but with so many great comics out there that are pushing the envelope of what comics can be, I think people are really missing the boat. My feeling is that if a publisher is not hiring the best possible artist and writer, giving

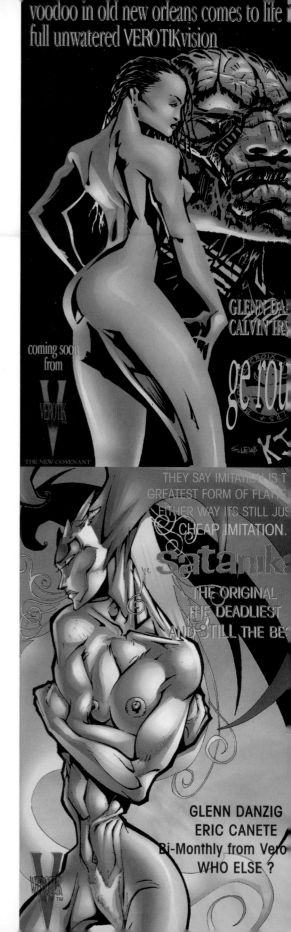

Opposite page, background:
Simon Bisley's art for a *Satanika* strip.

Opposite page, top right:
An advert, drawn by E. Lewis and "KJ" for Glen Danzig and Calvin Irving's 1997 *Ge Rouge* voodoo horror series. Danzig adapted and directed a film version in 2008.

Opposite page, bottom right:
A Verotik in-house ad for the bi-monthly flagship title, *Satanika*, written by Glen Danzig and distinctively drawn by Eric Canete and E. Lewis.

Right:
Stan Shaw's distinctive and sensuous art on *Sunglasses After Dark* #3, adapted by Nancy A. Collins from her own 1989 vampire novel.

them artistic freedom, and backing them with quality production, why bother?"

Several other horror/erotica publishers also launched around the same time, including Carnal Comics, which published its first titles in 1992. Tim Vigil's younger brother Joe co-created Calavera for Carnal, about a vigilante killing rapists and sexual predators.

These sexploitation comics are certainly not for everyone, but they have defiantly carved a substantial niche for themselves over the last 15 years by mixing a successful blend of sex and death for a hardcore generation. Yet many of these titles would cause the authorities to shriek in terror and unleash the full weight of the law against the retailers selling them.

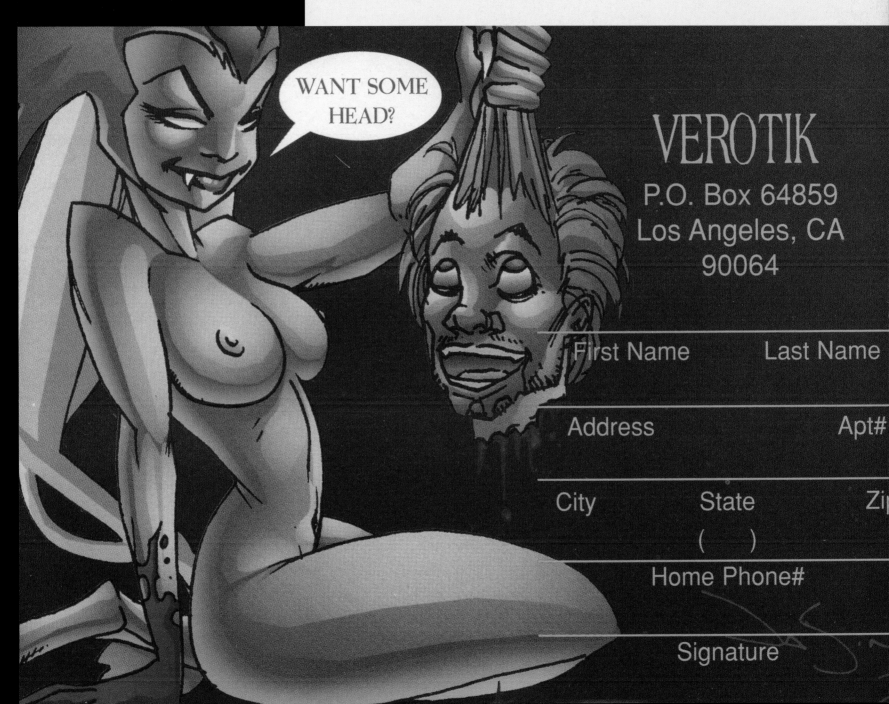

THE COMIC BOOK LEGAL DEFENSE FUND

The rise of erotic comics in specialist comic stores caused many local law enforcement agencies and states across America to become wary of this seemingly new and threatening genre. One victim of this mistrust was Michael Correa, the manager of Chicago's Friendly Frank's comics shop. In 1986 Correa was convicted of possession and sale of obscene materials for selling Kitchen Sink Press' *Bizarre Sex, Omaha the Cat Dancer*, and other titles. As the publisher, Denis Kitchen felt responsible to fight the verdict. He organized a fund raiser, which saw over $20,000 put toward hiring First Amendment litigator Burton Joseph. Ultimately Correa was acquitted, and Kitchen used the remaining money to set up a permanent nonprofit group to help defend against similar injustices. He established the Comic Book Legal Defense Fund (CBLDF) in 1986 and served as its president for its first 18 years, establishing the Fund as an organization "dedicated to the preservation of First Amendment (freedom of speech) rights for members of the comics community."

But with limited resources the CBLDF has also experienced failures in the past. In 1994, *Boiled Angel*, a self-published comic that deliberately tested the boundaries of acceptability with gruesome depictions of child abuse and cannibalism, was declared obscene by a Florida jury. The underground comics creator Mike Diana was put on a three-year probation, ordered to avoid all contact with children under 18, undergo psychological testing, enroll in a journalistic ethics course, pay a $3,000 fine, and perform 1,248 hours of community service. Even more unbelievably, he was forbidden to draw comics, with his residence subject to random inspections to make sure he didn't create any further comics. The CBLDF petitioned for a U.S. Supreme Court hearing, but was turned down. In 1995 the CBLDF also helped an Oklahoma shop, Planet Comics, through a two-year long battle involving Glenn Danzig's *Verotika* comics, but the owners, under intense financial

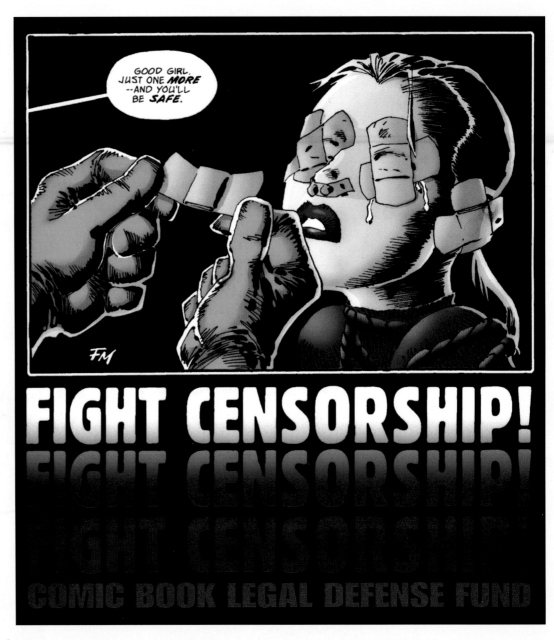

and emotional strain, decided to plead guilty to felony charges of trafficking in obscenity.

But things haven't all been bleak. In 2004 the CBLDF successfully fought the actions of U.S. Customs in South Carolina, which seized issues of the Slovenian anthology *Stripburger* on the somewhat dubious grounds of copyright

infringement. Specifically, one story, *Moj Stub* by Bojan Redzic, featured *Peanuts* characters. Another, *Richie Bush*, was a satirical anti-President attack which Peter Kuper created in the form of a *Richie Rich* parody. Despite the climb-down, it was clear to see there was a political motivation behind the seizure.

Opposite page:
Sin City creator, Frank Miller, drew this powerful and disturbing statement on censorship, which was created especially for the Comic Book Legal Defense Fund, and was turned into a T-shirt.

Right:
Artist Howard Cruse's 1995 drawing, *An Idea Imprisoned* (aka *Image Behind Bars*), was based on one of cartoonist Mike Diana's originals from his illegal *Boiled Angel* comic. It was done in protest to Diana's persecution and subsequently successful prosecution by Florida authorities in 1994.

IMAGE BEHIND BARS
BASED ON DRAWING
BY MIKE DIANA

In 2002, Charles Brownstein, a former comics journalist and events director of the San Diego Comic-Con, became Executive Director of the CBLDF. Two years later Chris Staros, publisher of *Top Shelf*, took over the presidency of the CBLDF from Denis Kitchen. Staros' passion for comics and freedom of expression equaled his predecessor and led him to publish one of the most important erotic comics to emerge in the last 10 years, *Lost Girls*, by Alan Moore and Melinda Gebbie. That same year saw the start of the CBLDF's longest running case. On Halloween, 2004, a Georgia comic shop owner, Gordon Lee, gave out copies of *Alternative Comics Sampler* as part of the nationwide Free Comic Book Day. Unfortunately it got into the hands of a 6-year-old whose parents complained to the police. Ironically it wasn't even an erotic comic that caused Lee all the problems, but rather a preview of the intelligent, sophisticated graphic novel *The Salon*, by Nick Bertozzi, about the birth of

Cubism in Paris. The "offensive" image was a scene of Picasso painting naked in his studio.

After three years of legal wrangling the CBLDF finally got to court in 2007, where the prosecution dramatically revealed that Lee had a previous conviction for selling a copy of a *Debbie Does Dallas* comic (published by Aircel between 1991-1992) to an adult. As it is illegal to mention previous convictions, the judge declared a mistrial. Despite initial threats to the contrary from the district attorney, the case was finally dropped altogether in April, 2008. As CBLDF founder Denis Kitchen pointed out, "Fortunately cases like Gordon Lee are still an aberration and not the norm...My concern is that every case like this one makes some retailers more nervous, particularly those in the Bible Belt, and thus even more cautious about carrying 'borderline' material. It's much easier for a retailer to quietly take preventive steps to avoid being 'the next Gordon Lee' than to be brave and carry the

full variety of material you ideally want your customers to be able to choose from."

Over the years the CBLDF has raised thousands of dollars to defend creators and retailers from prosecution by selling exclusive editions of books, prints, and t-shirts, and has been supported by practically every major comic creator from Frank Miller and Neil Gaiman on down. Gaiman currently sits on the advisory board alongside scriptwriter Peter David, DC Comics' publisher and president, Paul Levitz, and owner of Diamond Comics Distribution, Steve Geppi.

Although Denis Kitchen has retired from the board himself, he remains passionate in his belief that comics deserve the same constitutional rights as adult literature, gallery art, and films. At the 2005 Eisner Awards (comics' Oscars) Kitchen made a passionate speech, paraphrasing Benjamin Franklin, warning, "If we don't hang together to support the Fund, surely we will hang separately."

THE MAINSTREAM MOVES IN: ENIGMA AND THE EXTREMIST

As more adult themes began to emerge in the independent publishers' comics, the mainstream "big two" superhero publishers, Marvel and DC, started to take notice, realizing there was an older comic readership that they weren't catering to. In 1993, DC editor Karen Berger established a new imprint under the banner Vertigo with a whole range of horror, fantasy, and quirky fiction titles aimed specifically at "mature readers."

One of Vertigo's earliest titles to be released was *Enigma*, written by Peter Milligan and drawn by Duncan Fegredo. Initially, the tale appeared to be an above-average story of superhero hijinx, but halfway through it took unexpected twist, examining the awakening homosexuality of the central protagonist, Michael Smith. This controversial storyline had not previously been examined in such explicit detail in a superhero comic. Admittedly, there had been ham-fisted attempts at introducing gay superheroes in the past — most notably Northstar in Marvel's *Alpha Flight* — but this was a more mature, sensitive, and explicit approach.

Milligan followed up *Enigma* with a more in-depth look at the varied aspects of sexuality with *The Extremist*. As the erotic thriller's villain Patrick points out: "there isn't one sex, or even two sexes, but a whole multitude…"

The story of the eponymous protagonist lurks in the erotic underworld of San Francisco's bathhouses, BDSM fetish clubs, and a secret sexual society, known as The Order. *The Extremist* acts as an enforcer/assassin, eliminating anyone who steps out of line or threatens to expose The Order. The series hops back and forth through time focusing on three people, Judy and Jack Tanner, and their neighbor Tony, and how *The Extremist* affects their lives.

When looked back at, it is clear that Milligan didn't have much firsthand experience of these "scenes," but the writer does expertly explore the lure of taboos and why people are drawn to their darker halves, and the secrets that are kept from themselves and others. There are serious ethical questions posed, in the same vein that De Sade and Crowley challenged society's mores. *The Extremist* remains Milligan's favorite series for Vertigo "because there is more work to be done on it."

Both these titles dealt with taboo subjects for a mainstream publisher, but were applauded for their handling of these subjects.

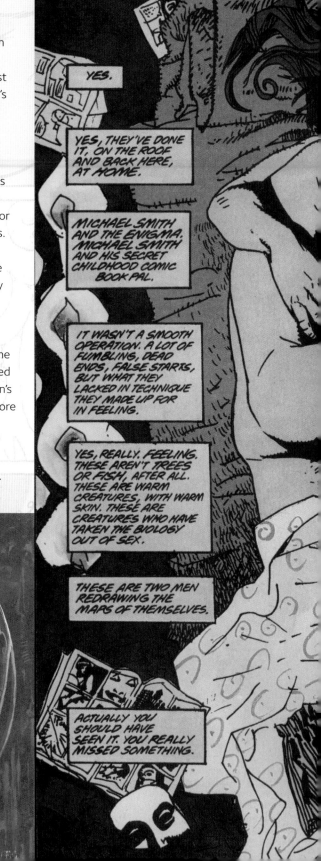

Opposite page, bottom left:
A panel drawn by John McCrea and Andrew Chiu from *Cruel and Unusual* #2. The four issue miniseries, written by Jamie Delano and Tom Peyer, dealt with exploitation TV, the electric chair, and the depravity of modern media.

Opposite page, bottom center:
Ted McKeveer's painting for the cover of his and writer Peter Milligan's *The Extremist* #4 (1993).

Left:
The first page of *Enigma* #7, drawn by Duncan Fegredo, when central protagonist Michael Smith has just had sex with superhero The Enigma. The series was one of the first mainstream comics to celebrate gay relationships in a healthy, positive—if convoluted—light.

Above:
The *Extremist*, Judy Tanner, in the foreground, is offered her ultimate fantasy in a Faustian bargain that threatens her soul and morality, in issue #1 (1993), drawn by Ted McKeever.

Right:
Dave Taylor's highly charged eroticism from Randy and Jean-Marc Lofficier's sex-based sci-fi series, *Tongue*Lash: The Hidden Place*, which was published by Dark Horse in 1999.

THE MAINSTREAM EXPANDS:
AMERICAN VIRGIN, PREACHER, AND THE PRO

Vertigo carried on its sexually themed titles with the 2006 *American Virgin* series, written by Steven T. Seagle and illustrated by Becky Cloonan. Seagle picked up on the US rise of teenagers pledging not to have sex before marriage, via the "Silver Ring Thing" set up in 1995, and explored its ramifications. The story follows Adam Chamberlain, a twentysomething born-again Christian preacher who struggles with his sexuality and faith. Chastely engaged to Cassie, the virgin Adam is forced to confront everything he believed in when his fiancée is seeming killed by terrorists in Africa. The young preacher goes to the "dark continent" and is plagued by erotic visions of Cassie and finally succumbs to his own carnal desires.

Referring to Vertigo's previous successes, Seagle confidently predicted that, "*American Virgin* will do for global sexual myth, history, and practice what *Preacher* did for gross-out action and *Hellblazer* did for demonology." The writer deliberately chose story arc names with sexual connotations such as *Head*, *Going Down*, *Wet*, and *Sixty-Nine*.

Garth Ennis and Steve Dillon's seminal series *Preacher* featured every kind of sexual predilection known to society, from mild bondage and cross-dressing through chicken fucking to fisting, yet did it all implicitly, rather than explicitly, and with heavy doses of humor, thus avoiding too many claims of gratuitousness. Nevertheless it still managed to irk more puritanical members of society.

But Ennis ramped up the sexual content with his superhero satire, *The Pro* — this time

published by Image — that followed the sexual misadventures of a superpowered streetwalker. Drawn by Amanda Conner and Jimmy Palmiotti, the one-shot graphic novel had its tongue planted firmly between two cheeks, as seen when a Superman-like hero ejaculates his sperm forcefully enough to knock a plane from the sky.

But as the mainstream and certain specialist erotic comic publishers seem to be merging to a center ground, there is increasing diversification into specific fetish comics and sexual niches. Today there's a whole raft of comics devoted to sections of society Middle America refused to believe even existed 50 years ago — and there are countless contemporary comics catering to the lesbian, gay, bisexual, and transgendered communities. As we will see in the next chapter, things certainly have come a long way from the puritanical anti-porn preaching of the mid-1950s.

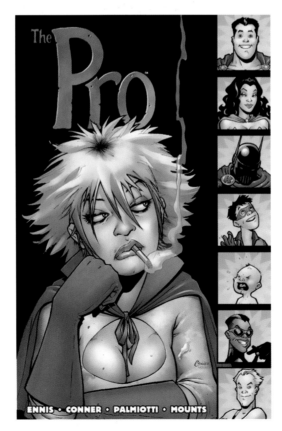

Harry's getting quite an eyeful.

Opposite page, bottom:
The cover to Garth Ennis, Amanda Conner, Jimmy Palmiotti, and Paul Mount's silly saga of a super-powered prostitute, *The Pro*.

Above:
A scene from Howard Chaykin and David Tischman's adult Vertigo series *American Century* #19. Set in the 50s, and drawn by Luke Ross and John Stokes, it evokes an Irving Klaw photo shoot, mixing the bizarre with the mundanity of daily life.

Left:
Pin-up artist Jim Silke's painting for the cover of *American Century* #21. Note the classic men's '50s magazines on the newsstand, such as *Hush!*, *Man*, and the infamous Bettie Page issue of *Eyeful*, are all real covers.

2

Gay and Lesbian Comix

In the history of arousing sequential art, the gay erotic comic is a relatively new subgenre, only making its presence felt in the late 1970s and early 1980s. Certainly, there were comics and cartoons with homosexual and lesbian themes — such as the *Tijuana Bible* featuring James Cagney in a gay orgy — but they were often written disparagingly from the outside looking in. Other, more sympathetic publications, such as the muscle mags of the '50s like *Physique Pictorial* (published by Bob Mizer), were more underground — catering to a then-secret subculture.

Mainstream society's tolerance toward homosexuality did not soften until the latter part of the 20th century and the lesbian, gay, bisexual, and transgender (LGBT) comics scene was inextricably linked with the Gay Liberation movement of the late 1960s/early 1970s. This also tied in with the rise of the more sexually liberated underground comics being produced in America and the combination saw the LGBT subgenre of comics blossom.

The first all-gay-male comic, *Gay Heart Throbs* #1, was published by Larry Fuller in 1976, and in typical underground comix style #2 wasn't released for another three years, in 1979. It was two further years before #3, but by then the wheels were in motion.

One of the earliest, and foremost, gay underground cartoonists was Howard Cruse. Raised in Springville, Alabama, in the 1950s, Cruse was the son of a preacher and his earliest cartoons appeared in *The Baptist Student* magazine, while he was still in school. He later contributed to *Fooey* and *Sick* — two *MAD*

That Night at the Stonewall
by Howard Cruse

magazine clones, the latter created by *Captain America* co-creator Joe Simon.

Cruse's cartooning first attracted national attention in the 1970s, when he contributed to various underground comix, including Denis Kitchen's *Bizarre Sex*. His best-known character was the eponymous Barefootz. He starred in a surreal series about a good-natured, well-dressed young man with large bare feet. Although dismissed by many underground fans as overly "cutesy," a term Cruse abhors, others found it a refreshing change from the more sexually and violently explicit comix of S. Clay Wilson and Spain Rodriguez. In 1969, while tripping out on acid, Cruse witnessed the infamous Stonewall Riot in New York, a milestone in the formation of the Gay Pride movement. The artist recounted the story in his 1982 strip, *That Night at the Stonewall*.

Opposite page, background:
A 2005 illustration by Howard Cruse.

Above left:
Wendel and his lover, Ollie, in a state of domesticated bliss, from the gay newspaper strip that ran in *The Advocate*.

Above right:
Howard Cruse recounts the infamous 1969 gay rights riot in New York in his autobiographical strip, *That Night at the Stonewall*.

Right:
One of Cruse's most well known characters, Wendel, relaxes at home.

In 1977, Cruse moved permanently to New York, where he met Eddie Sedarbaum, who would become his life partner in 1979. That same year Cruse, who had begun injecting gay themes in his underground comix throughout the 1970s without explicitly examining his own sexuality, was asked by Denis Kitchen to set up a new underground anthology. He founded and edited *Gay Comix*. The title featured work by openly gay and lesbian cartoonists, and was an important landmark title for gay creators. It helped them gain a voice about issues and subjects that related specifically to the LGBT community.

For much of the 1980s, Cruse created *Wendel*, an ongoing one- or two-page strip about an idealistic gay man, and his lover Ollie. Serialized in the gay magazine *The Advocate*, Cruse used the creative freedom of language and nudity to address important issues like AIDS, gay rights demos, gay-bashing, and closeted celebrities with a mixture of indignation and wit. A much-loved series, *Wendel* was subsequently collected into three volumes. Cruse spent the first half of the '90s creating *Stuck Rubber Baby*, a 210-page graphic novel for DC Comics' Paradox Press imprint in 1995. The semi-autobiographical story told of Toland Polk, a young white man growing up in the American South in the 1960s, simultaneously dealing with his awakening homosexuality and racial injustice. The multi-award-winning (including an Eisner and a Harvey) book was Cruse's longest, most serious work, which also included his most detailed and realistic art, using detailed crosshatching and stippling techniques and 12-panel heavy pages.

"After years spent drawing a comic strip like *Wendel*, set as it was in the post-Stonewall gay subculture of Gay Pride parades and lesbian softball, it seemed likely to be a refreshing change of pace to venture back to the complicated social currents that created so much turmoil down in Alabama during my high school and college years," explained Cruse. "In particular, I never addressed racism directly in *Wendel* because I feared trivializing the many issues that swirled around the central skin-color bugaboo. And of course, there was always that homophobic self-hatred of mine to shine a light on."

Today, Cruse remains an incredibly prolific and hugely inspirational figure for the legions of gay comic creators who have emerged since the launch of *Gay Comix*, many of whom weren't even born when it was first appeared.

Opposite page, top left:
Howard Cruse's autobiographical *Homoeroticism Blues* reveals the creator's difficulties and frustrations in being pigeonholed as a "gay artist."

Opposite page, top right:
A scene from Cruse's award winning, semi-autobiographical 1998 graphic novel, *Stuck Rubber Baby*.

Opposite page, bottom left:
Another raw, emotive page from *Stuck Rubber Baby*. The story was set in the Deep South in the 1960s and explored major taboos, such as interracial homosexuality.

Opposite page, bottom right:
Stuck Rubber Baby's central protagonist Toland Park in a sexually awkward moment.

GAY COMIX

Denis Kitchen was already a well established underground comix writer, editor, cartoonist and publisher—with such successful titles as *Bizarre Sex* and *Dope Comix*—when he approached creator Howard Cruse to launch a new anthology, *Gay Comix*. The comic would prove a turning point for Cruse, "I came out professionally in 1979 as part of the process of soliciting work for *Gay Comix*. Since we were just starting *Gay Comix* at that time, I took that occasion to indicate that I was more than just some liberal doing his bit to help out the downtrodden. It was important for the credibility of the title that I be clear about being gay myself," explained the artist in a 1998 interview with *Gayleauge.com*. "The cartoonists we were trying to find had to know that there would be a gay editor in charge who would understand where they were coming from."

Cover text:
oward Cruse
oberta regory
GAY Comix no. 6
Tim Barela
Trina Robbins

Adults $2.00

I WONDER IF ANYONE HERE KNOWS WE'RE GAY?

DARLIN', HOW COULD THEY TELL?

ENOUGH IS ENOUGH IS ENOUGH

Opposite page, bottom left:
Editor and cartoonist Robert Triptow's excellently subtle cover to *Gay Comix* #11 (1987). Note the fruit shapes and the T-Shirt legend, "We are everywhere."

Opposite page, right:
Howard Cruse's brutally honest *Billy Goes Out* strip from *Gay Comix* #1, which revealed the cruising scene in New York pre-AIDS. The artist described publishing the strip as "a little like inviting your mother to come in and watch you masturbate!"

Left:
The late Jerry Mills's colorful cover to *Gay Comix* #6 (1985) featuring the cast from his popular strip, *Poppers*. Mills passed away in 1993, tragically, from HIV complications, aged just 41.

Cruse sent out a call for submissions stating, "We're starting this book, and we're sending this letter to everyone because we don't know who's gay and who's not. If you're gay, or you have cartoonist friends who are gay, please give this to them — we'd really like to have good people for this book." And Cruse got them. There were very few openly gay cartoonists at the time, but Cruse invited Roberta Gregory and Mary Wings, as they had already come out in their previous work, and more importantly, he wanted the project to be "a co-gendered project. [he] didn't want a strictly male book." Renowned underground cartoonist Lee Marrs also joined, as well as Rand Holmes, heterosexual creator of the counterculture favorite *Harold Hedd*. Holmes drew the first issue's cover, which proudly announced, "Lesbians and Gay men put it on paper!"

Cruse's strip in the first issue, *Billy Goes Out*, was a milestone, "I was a little scared while I was doing it, because it was pretty frank about that backroom bar scene, and the sex was, like, really in your face. I mean, literally! Putting stuff like that on paper was a little like inviting your mother to come in and watch you masturbate! Crumb and the other undergrounders had done lots of sex stuff, but this was gay sex, and that always gets looked at differently. And what were my readers gonna think about me?"

Left:
The cover to *Gay Comix* #12 (1988), by Brad Parker, makes an amusing commentary on effeminate gay men and butch lesbians.

Opposite page:
Major Power and Spunky, an above-average gay *Captain America* parody strip written by Mal Coney and drawn by Sean Doran that appeared in *Buddies* and *Gay Comix*.

Gay Comix became a clarion call for cartoonists who hadn't previously been open about their homosexuality in their sequential art, and a new generation of gay and lesbian artists and writers emerged and flourished. As Cruse wrote in his editorial for issue #2, "The goal is to share our authentic selves, however perceptive, however flawed."

The gay bookstores supported the comix anthology and further issues were released on a tortuously slow schedule of one per year.

Of course, AIDS became a major factor in the gay scene and by the fourth issue of *Gay Comix*, in 1984, Cruse felt that the anthology could no longer avoid the issue and wrote and drew a sensitive strip, *Safe Sex*, which followed up on his Billy character from issue #1.

After four issues — and wanting to get back to more personal projects, like his *Wendel* strip — Cruse passed the reigns of *Gay Comix* on to fellow contributor and cartoonist Robert Triptow. "Editing a book involves a huge amount of correspondence. It was a very time-consuming thing, but it was never seriously income-producing," Cruse explained. Triptow (and his successor, Andy Mangels) attempted to increase the frequency of publication, with varying degrees of success.

Gay Comix changed its name to *Gay Comics*, signifying the switch from an underground publication to mainstream acceptance with #15, after Mangels took over the editorship with #14. He remained editor for eight years, and 10 issues, overseeing contributions from such gay comic stars as Donna Barr, Jeff Krell, Tim Barela, Alison Bechdel, and P. Craig Russell, as well as German cartoonist, Ralf König. *Gay Comics*' last issue, #25, was released in 1998, and the series remains a fondly remembered and important, if erratic, publication.

TOM OF FINLAND

Despite the success of *Gay Comix* in reaching a broader audience and gaining acceptance in society, there were actually gay comics and cartoonists serving the underground LGBT community long before. The US "Muscle" or "Beefcake" magazines of the 1950s masqueraded as sports and physical exercise publications, but were essentially gay pin-up magazines. Titles like *Physique Pictorial, Vim, Tomorrow's Man*, and *American Manhood* featured covers by quality draftsmen like George Quaintance and Etienne (aka Dom Orejudos) who drew lavish homoerotic fantasies featuring chiseled, toned gods oiling each other down. But one artist — who would become synonymous with gay erotica and comis — outshone them all, Touko Laaksonen, much better know as Tom of Finland.

Unsurprisingly, Laaksonen was born in Finland in May 1920. Growing up in the wilds, Laaksonen was surrounded by rough farmers, loggers, and frontiersmen and these would have a profound effect on his creative and emotional life. Raised by his teacher-parents, he loved art, literature, and music and was playing the piano and drawing comic strips by the age of five.

Aged 19, Laaksonen went to Helsinki to study advertising at art school. His lure toward men expanded to sexy city types that he found in the cosmopolitan port, such as construction workers, sailors, and policemen, themes that would feature heavily in his work. When Russia invaded Finland, Laaksonen was drafted into the army as a lieutenant. In the World War II blackouts Laaksonen experienced his first sexual encounters, with German soldiers in their smart uniforms. After the war, Laaksonen continued studying art and the piano, but with gay sex now a rarity, Laaksonen returned to his teenage habit of masturbating over his self-drawn homoerotic fantasies.

He did freelance artwork during the day, and at night played the piano at parties and cafes, joining Helsinki's bohemian set. He avoided the fledgling gay scene because it was dominated by the flamboyant effete queens, who had no appeal to the macho-loving artist. Laaksonen traveled regularly and frequented the gay cruising scenes in nearly every major city in Europe, but in 1953 he met Veli, a fellow Finn who would become his partner for the next 28 years.

At the end of 1956, a friend suggested Laaksonen should send his erotic artwork to *Physique Pictorial*, a popular US muscle magazine. Believing his Finnish name was too complex for Americans he signed them simply "Tom." The artwork was an instant hit and appeared on the cover of the spring 1957 issue. It featured a blond laughing lumberjack, drawn by "Tom of Finland" and a legend was born.

Opposite page, top right:
Two typically toned petrol pump attendants prepare to provide full service in 1972's *Kake: Service Station* minicomic by Tom of Finland.

Opposite page, bottom right and below:
Tom of Finland's closest artwork to a traditional comic page featuring Mike, circa 1965. The character's original Finnish masculine name, Vicky, was changed for the US market.

Right:
A penciled cover to the very first Kake story, *The Intruder*, from 1968. Note, the character's name is made from two erect penises.

kake

Tom had always drawn sequential strips — or "dirty drawings" as he called them — as far back as 1946. He developed his erotic 20-page mini-comics, with one panel per page, giving them to friends. His stories, undoubtedly inspired by his cruising years, involved various homoerotic stereotypes, from sailors and bikers to policemen and pin-striped office workers, picking each other up for intense, and always happy, sexual encounters. He was encouraged to carry on these strips in *Physique Pictorial* and by 1965 was looking for an ongoing character to base his vignettes around. After experimenting with the blonde Mike and Jack, he finally settled on the leather-clad biker, Kake, in 1968, published by the Danish company DFT and subsequently by Coq and Revolt Press in Sweden.

Despite his popularity in the United States, erotic and homosexual art still didn't pay very well and it wasn't until 15 years after he was first published before Tom of Finland could to quit his day job in advertising and concentrate full-time to his erotic art.

In 1973, Tom's first art exhibition, in Hamburg, Germany, turned into a disaster when all but one of the pictures were stolen. Badly bruised by the experience, it would be another five years (in 1978) before Tom would hold another exhibition, this time in Los Angeles, which surprisingly was his first trip to America. The introverted Helsinki artist soon became an international gay celebrity, with such friends as the erotic photographer Robert Mapplethorpe. In 1979 Tom became business partners with Canadian-American Durk Dehner, and two years later, in 1981, Tom's lover, Veli, died of throat cancer. Throughout the 1980s, Tom began

splitting his time between L.A. with Dehner and Helsinki, but at the age of 68 the artist was diagnosed with emphysema and was forced to reduce his traveling.

When the disease made his hand tremble too much, Tom switched to working in pastels, creating a series of color nudes until he died on 7 November 1991 from an emphysema-induced stroke.

Tom's work helped change the gay world's self-image, from pale shadows of women to strong, healthy, masculine sun-worshippers in boots and leather. This "social engineering" via his art was Tom's plan from the beginning, consciously striving to show homosexuality in a positive, upbeat, and open light. "I work very hard to make sure that the men I draw having sex are proud men having happy sex!"

His legacy lives on in the Tom of Finland Foundation set up by the artist and Dehner in 1984, initially to archive all his work. Since then the non-profit organisation has undertaken the noble and monumental task of promoting and preserving erotic works of art.

Opposite page:
A selection of scenes from the 20-page *Kake* story, *Cock-Hungry Cops*, originally published in 1968. Despite the apparent molestation, no one is ever really hurt, or looks particularly distressed in Tom's erotic fantasy world.

RALF KÖNIG

Born in August 1960, in Soest, Westphalia, König came out as a gay cartoonist in 1979, when he created his *SchwulComix* (which translates as Gay Comics) strip about the gay scene, in various underground comic magazines such as *Zomix* and the gay periodical *Rosa Flieder*. In 1981, he enrolled at the Academy of Fine Arts in Düsseldorf, studying for five years. In the first of these years, three collected works appeared, *Sarius, Das Sensationelle Comic Book,* and *SchwulComix*.

Bizarrely, in 1983, he was commissioned to create the series *Bodo und Heinz* for the snappily named magazine *Arbeit und Sicherheit im Deutschen Bergbau* (Work and Safety in German Coalmines), and the strip ran for two years.

With the publication of *SchwulComix 2,* in 1984, by Rosa Winkel, König finally found his own style. Inspired by French cartoonist Claire Bretécher's minimalist art, König created a series of satirical vignettes of the daily life of gay culture. Another two volumes of *SchwulComix* appeared in 1985 and 1986 (reprinted as *Silvestertuntenball*, aka The Queer's New Year's Party, and *Sahneschnittchen*, or Creamslice) and König was to become recognized as an important chronicler of gay culture.

In the English-speaking world, König's best known work is *Kondom des Grauens* (*The Killer Condom*) created in 1987. The parody detective story spawned a sequel, *Bis auf die Knochen* (*Until Blood Flows*) in 1990. 1987 also saw the release of *Der Bewegte Mann* (*Maybe, Maybe Not,* aka *Most Desired Man* or *The Turbulent Man*). It was König's mainstream breakthrough title and brought him to the attention of the wider public. There was a follow-up a year later, *Pretty Baby and Der Bewegte Mann*, which was made into a movie in 1994 with over 6.5 million German cinemagoers seeing it. It became the country's second most successful film to date. In fact, many of his books have been adapted for the silver screen in Germany.

Below, right, and opposite page:
Ralf König's modern sex comedy, *Maybe, Maybe Not* (aka *Pretty Baby* in Germany), sees the masculine, and seemingly straight, Axel move in with gay activist Norbert Brummer and cross-dressing Walter when his girlfriend kicks him out.

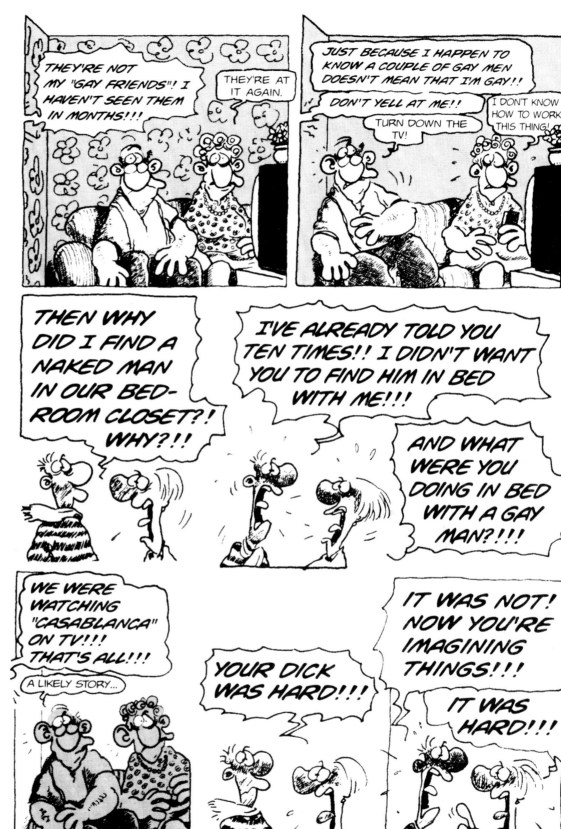

König continued to broaden his
creative horizons and — in the tradition of
Picasso and Aubrey Beardsley — adapted
Aristotle's sex comedy, *Lysistrata*, and paid
homage to Tom of Finland with his book
Safere Zeiten (1988). König's stories often
feature the potato-nosed couple, Konrad and
Paul, as the central protagonists (originally
created for the gay magazine *Magnus* in
1990) and the cartoonist continues to
recount their chronicles of everyday gay life.

Always a political animal, König
tackled the sensitive topic of AIDS in *Super
Paradise* (1999), and gay marriage in *Sie
Dürfen Sich Jetzt Küssen* (*You May Now
Kiss*). His blend of humor and passionate plots
has helped spread the message of tolerance
toward gays and lesbians, and in 1989 König
created eight comics for the German AIDS
Prevention Society.

Despite his wide-ranging success, the
'90s also saw criticism and lawsuits from the
conservative Bavarian youth authorities. In
the same year that he won Germany's highest
comics award—1992's Max und Moritz-Prize
for "Best German Comic Artist"—König's
book *Bullenklöten!* (*Bull's Balls!*) was deemed
harmful to young people. However, the case
was dismissed due to the book's artistic
content. Yet another investigation was
launched by the German state of Meiningen's
public prosecutor in 1996. It involved the
confiscation of comics from over 1,000 shops
across Germany, including *The Killer Condom*

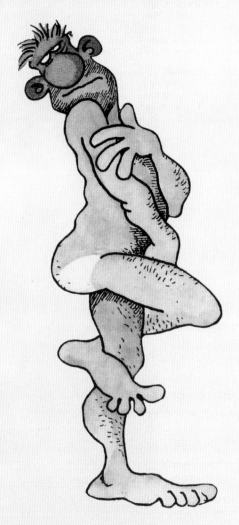

and—bizarrely—Art Spiegelman's Holocaust memoir, *Maus*. Typically, any obscenity trial failed to materialize, but the heavy-handed authoritarian intimidation is reminiscent of the tactics used on comic shops in the USA by an overzealous establishment.

2004 saw König create the anthropomorphic series *Roy & Al* about two dogs who belong to a gay couple. During 2005 and 2006 he wrote his biggest work to date, the two-volume *Dschinn Dschinn*, which dealt with the phenomenon of radical Islam. König also draws short stories for the monthly gay magazine *Männer Aktuell* and the French adult humor anthology *Fluide Glacial*. His books have been translated into 14 languages and sold almost seven million copies so far, making him the world's most popular author of gay fiction.

PATRICK FILLION

Alongside Joe Phillips, Patrick Fillion is possibly one of the most renowned of the new wave of homoerotic comic artists. Born in Quebec, Canada, in 1973, Fillion began drawing comic book art and nudes at a very early age. Growing up in a small Catholic community didn't make things easy, but Patrick persisted in illustrating the male form. When Fillion moved to Vancouver and discovered the gay community he became increasingly comfortable with his sexuality and began pushing the artistic envelope with his work, moving from slightly homoerotic to more uninhibited hardcore comics.

Having been inspired by US comic books at an early age, Fillion was no stranger to the superhero genre and he began incorporating these themes into his work, with strong gay overtones — superheroes in skin-tight costumes, barely concealing huge phalluses, which hark back to Tom of Finland's uniformed hunks. Fillion and his partner, Fraser, set up their own publishing company, Class Comics, and released humorous erotic comics like *Camili-Cat*, "a sexy Felinoid 'bottom' [submissive] who can't seem to get enough hardcore sex," who originally appeared in the *Meatmen* gay comics anthology; and *Naked Justice*, "a daring superhero with a minimalist approach to fashion and a very large and unique weapon." Other Fillion titles included *Satisfaction Guaranteed* and his popular *Boytoons*. Class Comics are published in France by H&O Editions, and Bruno Gmunder—Joe Phillips' publisher—released four of Fillion's art books; *Heroes*, *Mighty Males*, *Hot Chocolate*, and *Bliss: The Art of Patrick Fillion*.

Fillion also illustrates the gay magazines *Black Inches*, *Latin Inches*, and *Torso* magazine. The reserved and private artist has always been a supporter of fellow gay creators and helps emerging artists to find their voice, through his blogs, Class Comics' anthology, *Boytoons* magazine, and *Artistic License*. In 2006 Class started publishing other gay creators such as Logan, Max, HvH, Mike, and Zan Christensen.

Above:
This *Camili-Cat in...The Djinns* strip by Patrick Fillion originally appeared in *Meatmen #25* in 2002.

Right, top:
Patrick Fillion continues Tom of Finland's homoerotic tradition of a surfeit of oversized phalli. ("In space no one can hear you cream.")

Right, center:
A sated Satan slumbers.

Right, bottom:
Fillion's permanently masked, but nude, crime fighter, Naked Justice.

Left:
Fillion's cheeky *Zahn in 5 Easy Steps* strip combines fantasy comics with extreme erotica, turning traditional themes on their head with a homoerotic approach.

Above:
Another adventure for alien sexplorer, *Camili-Cat in The Game*.

ERIC SHANOWER, P. CRAIG RUSSELL, CRAIG HAMILTON, AND PHIL JIMENEZ

Possibly the four most famous openly gay artists working in mainstream comics today are Eric Shanower, P. Craig Russell, Craig Hamilton, and Phil Jimenez. All—with the exception of Jimenez—have contributed stories to *Gay Comix*, while also creating more conventional comics for publishers like Marvel and Dark Horse. Russell is renowned for his successful adaptations of classic operas, Michael Moorcock novels, and Oscar Wilde's *Fairy Tales*, as well as working with Neil Gaiman on the homoerotic *Murder Mysteries* graphic novel. His delicate, romantic artwork has won him both a Harvey and Eisner Award, and he came out to the industry in an interview with *The Comics Journal* in 1991, when he described himself as "Just another left-handed, night-dwelling, gay libertarian cartoonist."

Eric Shanower has adapted many of Frank L. Baum's *Oz* stories into graphic novels, and has since self-published his epic retelling of the Trojan War in his *Age of Bronze* series and graphic novels. "I came to terms with being gay... in late 1987. It then took me a year or so to let family and friends know. Before the San Diego Comic-Con in 1989, Andy Mangels, the Gays in Comics panel coordinator, phoned and very judiciously asked me whether I'd have any interest in being on the panel since he'd heard from a mutual acquaintance who wished to remain anonymous that I might be gay. I was flattered to be asked to appear on a panel, and I thought I could set a positive example, so I agreed to appear," Shanower revealed in an online interview. "I'm not sure how it's affected my career. I guess I wouldn't have had a story in *Gay Comix*... Perhaps I've met some people because I'm gay who I might not have met otherwise, or editors have thought of calling me for a job because I was in a certain place at a certain time somehow having to do with my being gay."

Craig Hamilton worked on the 1986 *Aquaman* miniseries for DC Comics. The artist's work wove an implicit homoeroticism into the story, with beautifully toned male torsos draped across the page. Both Wonder Woman and Aquaman have always been incredibly popular superheroes in the gay community, possibly because of the glamor and beefcake that each character exudes, and Hamilton's art certainly played up the latter. As Phil Jimenez noted, "DC is a very gay-friendly company. They always have been."

Coming to comics slightly later than the others, Phil Jimenez has flourished in mainstream comics. He was born and raised in Los Angeles, but moved to New York City to attend the School for Visual Arts. After graduating at 21, he got a job working for Neil Pozner, DC Comics' creative director. "He was probably my greatest mentor at DC Comics. He was an incredibly talented man, with some very strong opinions about the way things should be done. I developed a crush on him the minute I met him..." recalled Jimenez, and the two became a couple—despite the 15-year age gap, and Pozner's HIV-positive status. They remained a couple until Pozner's tragic death from AIDS-related illnesses in 1994. "Nobody at DC knew that we were together. They just knew that we were really good friends..." In 1996, Jimenez wrote and drew the *Tempest* miniseries, based on a character from Pozner's earlier *Aquaman* series. In the last issue, Jimenez wrote an editorial, dedicating the series to his late partner and publicly outing himself, the first creator to do so in a mainstream comic. "It got over 150 letters," the creator revealed, "including the classic letter from the kid in Iowa: 'I didn't know there was anyone else like me.' That's what counts. It meant a lot to people." Since then Jimenez has gone on to work on many huge projects, such as *Wonder Woman* and *Infinite Crisis*, and continued working on LGBT themes with a short story in Vertigo's *Heartthrobs* anthology written by Robert Rodi, and in Grant Morrison's *The Invisibles*, which featured a transvestite lead character, Lord Fanny.

Opposite page, bottom right:
The Myth of Hycynthus/Hycinthus (sic), written and penciled by David Sexton and inked by P. Craig Russell from *Gay Comix* #21 (1994). The story recounted the ancient Greek gay love story between Hyacinthus and Apollo, the sun god.

Above:
Craig Hamilton and Tony Harris' pin-up of lesbian vampire lovers from the back of *Gay Comix* #18 (1993).

Right:
Heartthrobs #1 (Vertigo/DC, January 1999) featured this gay romance story, *Genes and a T-Shirt*, by Robert Rodi and Phil Jimenez. In the satirical story, a homosexual has a medical procedure to stop him being gay, with the expected failure.

DESERT PEACH & DONNA BARR

Born in 1952 in Washington state, Donna Barr served in the US Army between 1970-73 and received a bachelors' degree in German from Ohio State University in 1978. Both elements would become strong influences in her work. *The Desert Peach*, Barr's series about the WWII adventures of Field Marshall Erwin Rommel's younger, fictional, gay brother, Pfirsich, is an exquisite piece of genre-busting work. Primarily set in the Afrika Korps, during 1940–1943, Manfred Pfirsich Marie Rommel is the understanding father figure to a gaggle of ne'er do well, would-be soldiers. "He is a man of integrity and peace thrust into a conflict he finds appalling," explained the writer/artist. In reality Rommel's youngest brother, Manfred, died in infancy, "So all I've done is pick up and let live a human being that the universe threw away."

The original three-issue miniseries was published by Thoughts & Images in October, 1988 and started out as a simple play on the color Desert Peach and Rommel Senior's nickname, The Desert Fox. "I couldn't resist the pun," explained the creator, in an interview with Ruth Saunders. "I was badly infected by *The Goon Show* [a BBC radio comedy series] as a callow child." But Barr was very careful to avoid obvious, crass clichés, "It's not 'Gay Nazis.' It's a WWII German officer, who is homosexual. Don't think in genres and sound bites if you're going to read the *[Desert] Peach*; you'll only confuse yourself."

The Peach has two weaknesses — his lover, Lieutenant Rosen Kavalier (whose real name is the less glamorous Melvin Gonville Ramsbottom) — and his Prussian-style uniform. "Riding breeches and boots do wonders for a man!" exclaimed Barr. *The Desert Peach* went on for 30-issue run and was collected into several books. The series also earned Barr a Xeric Award and Grant in 2002 to help her continue self-publishing.

Barr even turned the series, fittingly, into *Desert Peach, The Musical* and praised the leading man, "Jon Winston Hauer, who played [Pfirsich] in the musical, is him to a T. Jon can even ride horses, and is, for all his delicate and pretty appearance, tremendously powerful..."

Barr's other work has included *Stinz* (1984), about a centaur who joins a pre-industrial Germanic army and has a hard time fitting in (like The Peach), *Hader And the Colonel*, and *Bosom Enemies*. Barr also examined another aspect of LGBT culture with *Barr Girls*, which was all about life in a hermaphroditic world, with the great tagline: "Just because everyone is one sex doesn't mean they're any more together than we are." Barr's books are now sold from Japan and Australia to Serbia, Croatia, and Slovenia, and she continues to pave the way for female comic creators.

The Wonder Look—
NOT just gender-limited any more...

24

Opposite page, top right:
A fashion sketch by Barr from 2006 and 2007. The top implies the ongoing link with super heroine Wonder Woman and the LGBT community, with the text, "The wonder look—not just gender-limited any more."

Opposite page, bottom right, and bottom left:
Interior pages from *The Desert Peach* reveal its erotic, sensitive, and humorous nature.

Top left:
Donna Barr's gauche pin-up of the Desert Peach's tank crew.

Top center:
This watercolour illustration of the traditional "Green Man" is given an erotic spin by Barr.

Bottom center:
A fully painted cover to *The Desert Peach*, by creator Donna Barr. It guest stars The Peach's elder brother, Erwin Rommel, The Desert Fox.

Bottom right:
Manfred Pfirsich Marie Rommel, The Desert Peach, is grabbed by his lover, Rosen Kavalier.

A.A.R.G.H CLAUSE 28 AND ALL THAT

Left:
David Shenton's funny strip, *Controlled Hysteria*, reveals the benefits of gay men in 1988's A.A.R.G.H, pointing out that Tchaikovsky and Michelangelo were both gay.

Opposite page, left:
Frank Miller's *Robocop* parody, *Robohomophobe*, from A.A.R.G.H, caused much controversy, as many saw the strip as homophobic as the British government's Clause 28.

Opposite page, right:
The League of Extraordinary Gentlemen artist, Kev O'Neill, drew this strip that ridiculed James Anderton, the then-Chief Constable for the Greater Manchester police. Anderson was openly swayed by his Christianity, publicly espousing anti-gay views and supporting Clause 28.

Staggeringly, homosexuality was illegal in the UK until 1967, when it was finally decriminalized for over 21 year-old men (lesbianism was never made illegal). But then, after 20 years of struggling to gain acceptance, the gay community was struck a blow, and tolerance hit an all-time low during Margaret Thatcher's Conservative government in the 1980s. The repressive cabinet introduced a controversial amendment to the Local Government Act — Clause 28 — in 1988 that prevented the education, discussion, or "promotion" of homosexuality by local authorities.

At that time, the comic book writer extraordinaire Alan Moore was in a relationship with his then-wife, and their girlfriend, and he felt that the law would obviously affect them personally. "[It was] sort of an…experimental relationship, I suppose you'd call it. It was something we were very serious about, and it endured for two to three years, which was a mark of that seriousness," explained Moore in an interview with *Newsarama* in 2004. "It was also around about that time that the government over here first proposed Clause 28…"

"That was the first kind of legislation over here in a long time that was aimed at one specific minority, which had more than a whiff of the Third Reich about it…" explained the Northampton writer. "It was very, very nasty — the implications of it were very serious."

Outraged at this discriminatory act, and to help raise money for the Organization for Lesbian and Gay Action (OLGA), Moore formed Mad Love—his own publishing company—and gathered up as many big names as possible and published a protest comic anthology, A.A.R.G.H (Artists Against Rampant Governmental Homophobia).

"We asked all of my friends in comics, or in some instances people who I never had contact with, but were very generous in offering work, and we put together a fairly stellar roster of talent very quickly." The anthology was an eclectic mix of work by Neil Gaiman, Bryan Talbot, Dave Sim, Frank Miller, Dave Gibbons, and many other big names in the industry. Moore contributed an eight-page story called *The Mirror of Love,* an overview of gay history drawn by Steve Bissette and Rick Veitch. "Having that idea of trying to come up with a history

of gay culture — I had eight pages to do it in," Moore said. "I did it with Steve…and Rick…who did a beautiful job on the comic strip between them, given the constraints of what we were trying to do in just eight pages…"

The officially-entitled "Section 28" became law on 24 May 1988 and schools and local authorities scrapped various programs for fear of prosecution. In 1994, there was a chink of light when a compromise amendment to the Criminal Justice and Public Order Act 1994 lowered the age of consent for homosexuals to 18 (it is 16 for heterosexuals in the UK). Finally, Clause 28 was eventually repealed in 2003, "So I guess it is a victory for common sense and human decency, even if it did take a long while in coming," said Moore.

The Mirror of Love was reworked as a book with gay Spanish illustrator and comics colorist, José Villarrubia for *Top Shelf.* Villarrubia performed the work on stage at numerous readings and called Moore's work "a love letter that is also a political manifesto," and "One of the most touching pieces that Alan has written and it has been an honor to turn it into an illustrated book."

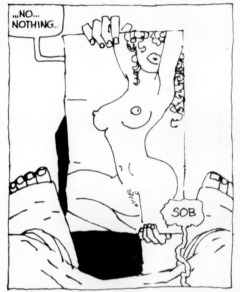

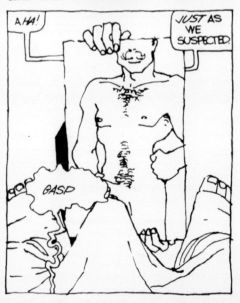

STANGROOM & LOWTHER: MEATMEN AND BUDDIES

The British duo of writer Howard Stangroom and artist Stephen Lowther were at the forefront of the gay comics scene throughout the '80s and '90s, being regular contributors to *Gay Comix*, *Meatmen*, and other gay titles.

They met in the baking British summer drought of 1976. "I was working at a pornographer's in Darlington, in the North East of England—we're both Yorkshiremen by birth. It was my first job out of reform school," joked Stangroom, in a 2005 interview. Stangroom's boss was trying to diversify, and wanted to produce a comics fan magazine. "I was one of the artists that stepped forward," explained Lowther.

The duo worked on many fan projects, but it wasn't until around 1980 that they started work on gay themes. Their stories were sexy, humorous, and thought-provoking, with a more inclusive range of ages and body types than the usual beefcake (big muscle men) and twinks (younger, lithe men). Their first strip for *Gay Comix #11*, *Second Chance?*, was a twist on the post-apocalypse-survivors-restart-the-world sci-fi story, replacing Adam and Eve with Adam and Steve.

Stangroom also helped launch and edit *Buddies*, alongside Don Melia — the co-editor of the 1988 AIDS charity comics anthology, *Strip Aids*. Sadly, Melia died of AIDS-related illnesses, and after issue #2 of *Buddies*, Stangroom continued the title for another four issues from 1993 to 1996. Stangroom recalled,"Don was trying to start a British version of *Gay Comix*, and we gave him the story *Can We Do It Until We Need Glasses?*, a true life adventure in Gutersloh, Germany. [It was the] first time I'd had myself as the star of a strip and, hey, I got lucky a couple of times after people saw me in the comic!"

Stangroom and Lowther's stories of "balls and brains" started appearing in *Meatmen #6*, a semi-annual gay comics paperback launched in 1986 by Winston Leyland. Starting out as a mixture of humorous and erotic strips, the title plunged into the latter, with later issues of

Meatmen consisting mostly of full frontal male nudity and sexual encounters. As *Gay Today* magazine remarked, *Meatmen* was packed full of "explicit erotic fantasy adventures with greater arousal power than any photographs in my memory."

Meatmen ran for 25 issues before the publication folded in 2005. Each book-sized issue was self-contained, but several creators and their characters became regulars, such as Zack, aka former *Dan Dare* illustrator Oliver Frey, whose tales of not-so-innocent boys in heat were perennial favorites. As was the late John Blackburn's Coley, a blond, buff, bisexual, "19-year old voodoo sexgod" who travels through space and time getting into the inevitable sexcapades. Other popular contributors included Belasco, Stepan Zubinski, Jeff Jacklin, and Patrick Fillion. However, the increased testosterone — and decreased intelligence — turned off the creative pair of Stangroom and Lowther, and their last contribution was in #15.

Stangroom has since contributed to Donna Barr's *Ersatz Peach* collection, *Avalon, Boy Crazy Boy, Heartbreak Hotel, Him, Joy of S*x*, and the slightly less homoerotic *Masters of the Universe* and *My Little Pony*. Much of his and Lowther's work was collected, in full-color for the first time, in the Bruno Gmünder paperback *Prime Cuts*, released in 2005. These days Stangroom, under his civilian name of Will Morgan, is the manager of the London comic shop, 30th Century Comics, based in Putney. Stephen Lowther works as a medical archivist in London.

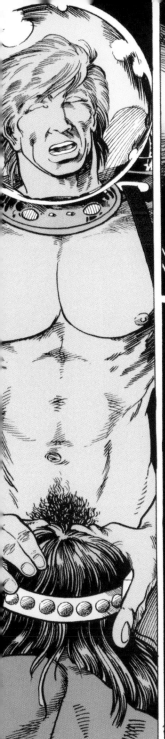

ROBERTA GREGORY AND LESBIAN CARTOONISTS

Running alongside the revolution in gay comix, lesbian sisters were also producing high-quality comics. While perhaps less defined as true erotica — with the intention of arousing the reader — lesbian sequential art is no less sexual in its content. Sexual politics play an important part of many of the strips. At the forefront of the dyke cartoonist movement was Roberta Gregory, who self-published 10,000 copies of the first lesbian-themed comic, *Dynamite Damsels*, in 1976, the same year *Gay Heart Throbs* was launched. The comic included two short stories: *Superdyke*, a lesbian super-heroine, and *Liberatia*, the story of a women-only land.

Gregory went on to create her most famous and funny character, the ever-angry-at-the-world Midge—better known as Bitchy Bitch—in her comic *Naughty Bits* #1, published by Fantagraphics, in March 1991. Gregory went on to create Bitchy's lesbian counterpart,

Butchy, who — as the artist put it, "Remembers the glory days of the early feminist movement, before 'those darn straight women' spoiled it for the rest of the dykes!" Gregory was asked to create Butchy for an anthology but managed to succeed in enraging and offending the commissioning editor!

Gregory then created the three-issue miniseries *Artistic Licentiousness*. Originally intended to be a "smutty" comic to cash in on the success of the Eros Comix line, it was the story of Denise, a writer who has just come out of a bad relationship with a man and decided she really prefers women, and Kevin, a comics creator. Each discovers that making assumptions about someone's sexuality — especially their own — is not a good idea. Unfortunately, the publisher, Starhead Comics, went bust, so Gregory self-published the last two issues, making them "less overtly sexual and more intriguing."

CHRIS, NOREEN HERE... CHRIS? ARE YOU JOINING US AT THE CLUB OR NOT? IT'S THE THIRD MESSAGE I'VE LEFT IN THE BLOODY MACHINE...

I'M WAITING FOR YOU, HONEY... ARE YOU GOING? ZERO!

Lesbian Pride

NO MEETING IN THE WORLD IS INTERESTING ENOUGH TO STOP SUCH BEAUTIFUL LOVEMAKING

OH CHRIS...

CHRIS... LET ME DO TO YOU WHAT YOU'VE JUST DONE TO ME

MMHHH SLOWLIER SUGAR... I DON'T WANT TO COME TOO EARLY...

SHE MADE GREAT LOVE TO ME, SWEET AND STRONG, THE BEST LOVE I'D HAD FOR MONTHS. I STILL QUAVER AT THE THOUGHT OF IT.

AAH.. AAAAHH..AH.. AH..

1 HOUR LATER CHRIS, I DON'T WANT TO UPSET YOUR RELATIONSHIP WITH NOREEN... NEVER MIND LOVE! THINGS WILL SETTLE DOWN IN A DAY OR 2!

WILL YOU TELL HER? NOPE. I DON'T THINK IT'S A GOOD IDEA!

WE JUST HAD AN ARGUMENT ABOUT POLY-MONO RELATIONSHIP, AND BELIEVE ME, I DON'T WANNA GO INTO IT AGAIN! UGH!

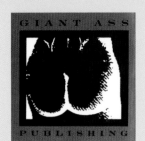

Another high-profile lesbian cartoonist with an angry creation is Diane DiMassa, whose *The Hothead Paisan* is a no-holds-barred reaction to the misogynist underground comix of the early 1970s. Born in 1959 in New Haven, Connecticut, DiMassa created her "homicidal lesbian terrorist..." as therapy while recovering from drug and alcohol addiction in 1991. Her uncompromising character had wild hair "and a fetish for guns, grenades, mallets, and sharp objects", used to avenge wrongs against women. Highly political, the comic is reminiscent of Spain's comix creation *Trashman*, who used over-the-top violence to get revenge on corporate and governmental miscreants. The series is narrated by the Paisan's cat (called Chicken) with a dry wit. The first 20 issues were published by the fantastically named Giant Ass Publishing and were collected into one volume by Cleis Press. DiMassa has also contributed to several gay comic anthologies and publications, including Robert Kirby's *Strange Looking Exile*, *Gay Comics*, *Frighten the Horses*, *The Advocate*, and *Oh*. She also collaborated with "Post Punk Porn novelist", Kathy Acker on *Pussycat Fever* in 1995.

Opposite page, top right:
Diane DiMassa's cover to *Hothead Paisan* #12 featuring the "Homicidal Lesbian Terrorist."

Opposite page, bottom left:
A scene from DiMassa's *Hothead Paisan* #12 reveals a rarely discussed female desire for hermaphrodites and transsexuals.

Opposite page, bottom right:
One of the original lesbian cartoonists to achieve great success was Roberta Gregory. This is the cover to her series, *Artistic Licentiousness*, which dealt with a myriad of sexual politics and mythological themes.

Left:
A page from Italian cartoonist Serena Pillai's *The Italian Cousin*, about holiday a romance between a "butch" and a "femme," from the first *Juicy Mother* anthology.

ALISON BECHDEL'S DYKES TO WATCH OUT FOR

Out of all the lesbian comics artists and cartoonists working today, the queen of them all is Alison Bechdel. Born 10 September, 1960, Bechdel was influenced by "gothic" cartoonists Charles Addams and Edward Gorey, *MAD* magazine and Norman Rockwell. "When I was 22, I picked up a copy of *Gay Comix*...and it was seeing [Cruse's] work there, along with stuff by other early gay and lesbian cartoonists like Mary Wings, Jennifer Camper, and Jerry Mills, that made me realize I could draw cartoons about my own queer life."

Duly inspired, Bechdel's groundbreaking newspaper strip, *Dykes To Watch Out For* (DTWOF), first appeared in *Womannews*, a New York newspaper, in July, 1983. "I liked [the title's] contradictory meanings,'Watch out for' as in 'seek out,' and 'watch out for' as in 'avoid,'" explained the artist/writer. "I worry about it from time to time because it's really kind of an unwieldy title. But not as unwieldy as Carbon-Based Beings To Watch Out For, which is really more accurate now that the characters aren't all lesbians."

Bechdel self-syndicated the strip in 1985, and the first collection was released in 1986. Since then the strip has become an LGBT institution in dozens of newspapers, been translated into several languages, and collected in a series of award-winning books.

In 2006, Bechdel's graphic novel memoir *Fun Home: A Family Tragicomic* was published by Houghton Mifflin, spending two weeks on *The New York Times*' Hardcover Non-fiction Best Seller list. The coming-of-age tale revealed the tragic story of Bechdel's coming out as a lesbian and her father's own repressed homosexuality, and has been called a "rare, prime example of why graphic novels have taken over the conversation about American literature."

In April, 2003 a non-profit organization was established to support LGBT comics. Prism Comics was initially set up by a small group of US comics fans and professionals who put together the annual *Out in Comics*, which listed

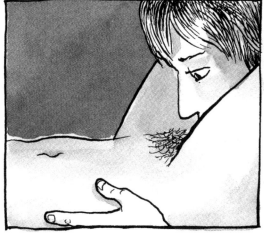

LGBT creators, but only lasted three issues. The volunteers decided to create Prism to provide services such as promotion and publicity of gay comics, via conventions and their website. The organization also produces the annual *Prism Comics: Your LGBT Guide to Comics*, which features creators' work, overviews of gay themes in comics, news, and features. On the advisory board sit most of the key names in LGBT comics, including Howard Cruse, Tim Fish, Andy Mangels, Lee Marrs, and Joe Phillips, among others. The group even awards a $1,000 grant each September to a comics creator who has published a work of interest to an LGBT audience.

Another entrant on the LGBT scene is the infrequent *Juicy Mother* anthology edited by Jennifer Camper. Bechdel, Leanne Franson, Howard Cruse, Diane DiMassa, Robert Kirby, Robert Triptow, and a host of other LGBT cartoonists have all contributed to it.

So the gay comics market has gone from practically nonexistent to a thriving sub-genre, with its own recognized charity, in just over 30 years, thanks to the determined and brave creators demanding their voices be heard through their sequential art.

Opposite page:
An erudite scene of self-discovery from Alison Bechdel's bestselling 2006 graphic novel, *Fun Home: A Family Tragicomic*.

Left:
The cover to the first collection of Bechdel's *Dykes To Watch Out For* strips.

Above:
Two *Dykes To Watch Out For* strips that reveal Bechdel's deft touch when discussing sexual subjects within a lesbian relationship, that does not descend into stereotypical male fantasies.

3

European Erotique

MILO MANARA

European erotic comics have always been far ahead of the United States and Great Britain in terms of sophistication and acceptability — particularly in Italy, where the renowned Latin lovers were one of the first countries to truly embrace and develop the erotic comic genre. At the forefront of this revolution was Milo Manara, an artist whose skill at drawing sensuous women and intensely arousing situations is unsurpassed.

Born in 1945, the Italian artist was heavily influenced by classical painters like Raphael and, as a boy, he even ran away from home to see an exhibition of work by the painter Giorgio di Chirico. He studied architecture and painting, but became intrigued by the emerging Italian underground comix, or fumetti, in the mid- to late 1960s. He made his comics debut in 1969 for *Genius*, a sexy noir comic book in the vein of *Kriminal* and *Satanik*. He worked for minor publications such as *Jolanda*, a softcore title, and the satirical magazine *Telerompo*, before he was hired by the boys' anthology *Il Corriere dei Ragazzi* to work with writer Mino Milani.

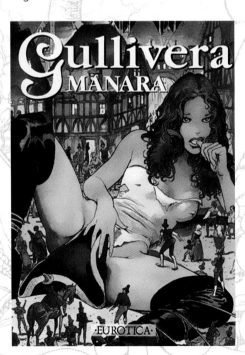

Previous page:
An exquisite self-portrait of Italian erotic artist, Giovanna Casotto, in the bath.

Background:
An illustration of cornucopia, or "horn of plenty," which also represents fertility.

Left:
Milo Manara's erotic adaptation of Jonathan Swift's classic novel changed the eponymous protagonist to a female in *Gullivera*.

Opposite page, top right and Above left:
An erotic scene from Manara and Hugo Pratt's award-winning graphic novel, *Indian Summer*, set in early colonial America. Here, the supposedly puritanical Reverend Black shows his true colors.

Opposite page, bottom right:
A scene from Manara's magic realist story *Trip to Tulum*, written by famed Italian film director, Federico Fellini. The director also guest stars in his own story, seen here in white.

Left:
A sexually "liberated" Irish prostitute reveals herself in Pratt and Manara's Argentine historical drama, *El Gaucho*.

Above:
This disturbingly devilish illustration from Manara treads a fine line by not actually revealing Satan's member.

FREEDOM, FREEDOM, WHAT DO YOU WANT TO DO WITH IT? SOUTH AMERICA IS OUT THERE. WHEN WE GO TO SHORE, ESCAPE AND GET YOUR FREEDOM.

OH SIR... I FEEL SOMETHING SWELLING UP.

THEY ARE PAPISTS LIKE YOU. I DON'T THINK THEY'LL EAT YOU. YOUR DESTINY IS TO SPREAD YOUR LEGS, THAT'S ALL. IT WILL SUIT THEM TOO, MOLLY. IN ANY CASE, I'LL SEE WHAT I CAN DO.

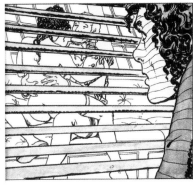

DAMN DIRTY PIGS!

Milo Manara's first graphic novel as an artist and writer was *HP and Giuseppe Bergman*, published in 1983. "HP" is Manara's friend, collaborator, and fellow Italian artist/writer legend, the late Hugo Pratt. Bergman had been created by Manara five years earlier (in 1978), for the French comics magazine *A Suivre*. The series became known for its combination of experimental narrative and explicit sex, and has been collected into six books so far.

Manara has since produced over 30 graphic novels and art books, including the four-part series *Il Gioco* (1983, translated as *Click*), about a device that renders women helplessly aroused at the flick of a switch, and *Il Profumo dell'invisibile* (1986, translated under the name *Butterscotch*), about the invention of a body paint that makes the wearer invisible. *The Ape*, serialized in the US magazine *Heavy Metal* in the early 1980s, retells the story of the Chinese Monkey King — with humor, arousing artwork, and political overtones.

Manara's stories generally revolve around elegant, beautiful women caught up in unlikely and fantastical erotic scenarios, and his art style favors clean lines for women, reserving more complex drawings for monsters or other supernatural elements. Many of his comics have themes of bondage, domination, humiliation, voyeurism, the supernatural, and the sexual tension lurking beneath various aspects of Italian society. Manara's work varies in explicitness, but the general mood is playful rather than misogynistic, and his skill in creating atmosphere as well as occasional excursions into more "mainstream" stories has helped give him an air of artistic respectability. His work has reached an American audience, largely through *Heavy Metal*, but curiously, Manara is less popular in Italy than in France, where he is considered one of the most important cartoonists in the world.

VITTORIO GIARDINO

Just one year younger than Manara, Vittorio Giardino was a latecomer to sequential art and was already 31 when he entered the comics scene in 1978. The Italian former electrical engineer was inspired by the Belgian ligne claire school of art that *Tin-Tin* creator Herge belonged to.

After creating his first comics for La Città Futura, Giardino created the character Sam Pezzo, a private investigator whose adventures appeared in comic anthologies, *Il Mago* and *Orient-Express* in 1981. The following year, after three collections, he abandoned Pezzo to work on the complex 1930s espionage stories of Max Fridman, in *Orient-Express and Hungarian Rhapsody*.

After 1986, he regularly featured in *L'Espresso*, and worked as an illustrator for Italian newspapers *La Repubblica* and *L'Unità*, and French magazine *Je Bouquine*.

Giardino's erotic comic output may be less than his Italian peers, but is no less important. He began illustrating short stories and covers for the erotic anthology *Glamour International*, and started his most famous work in the English language, *Little Ego*, in 1984. This series of short stories continued in *Comic Art* and was originally an erotic homage to Winsor McCay's beloved *Little Nemo* newspaper strip, with a beautiful female protagonist replacing the little boy, Nemo. Little Ego's sexual dreams increase in frequeny until a longer, ongoing narrative develops, as she experiences every sexual fantasy, from an orgy with multiple versions of herself to bestiality with a crocodile! The strips were collected in 1989 and the book has remained in print ever since, remaining a benchmark of quality comic book erotica.

In 1986 *Glamour* produced a collection of Giardino's erotic illustrations and in 1989 his collection of dangerous holiday romances, *Vacanze Fatali* (*Fatal Holidays*, translated as *Deadly Dalliance in America*) was released. Shortly after, he released a follow up, *Dream Journeys*, and then teamed up with writer Giovanni Barbieri to create the racy "soap opera" comic, *Eva Miranda*.

"Women fascinate me in real life, before I even start drawing, and it's as much a pleasure to draw them as it is to know them," Giardino explained in a 2006 interview with *Libero*. "I have no intention to push the erotic elements [of my comics] beyond my own clear boundaries, for one simple reason. For years I have had adolescent daughters in the house and they are convinced that the eroticism is not about the body, but rather the mind."

Opposite page:
Giardino's ligne claire art style is deeply arousing and Little Ego's dream adventures all have strongly overt Freudian metaphors.

Left:
The Italian artist's page layouts and final panels were a direct homage to Winsor McCay's *Little Nemo* strip.

Above:
A new sketch that appeared in the 2006 US edition of *Little Ego*.

PAOLO E. SERPIERI

Serpieri, like his Italian peers, is an erotic comics artistic genius whose reputation has spread far beyond his native homeland. Born in Venice in 1944, Paolo Eleuteri Serpieri studied painting and architecture at the Fine Art Academy in Rome under Renato Guttuso. By 1966, critics were lauding his fine art paintings, but nine years later, in 1975, the artist had forgone this career in exchange for the medium he would truly excel in, comics.

He teamed up with writer Raffaele Ambrosio, and together they created a series of Westerns (a perennially popular comics genre in Italy), including *L'Indiana Bianca* (*The White Indian*); *L'Uomo di Medicina* (*Medicine Man*); and the historical *L'Histoire du Far-West* (*The Story of the West*), which were published in the magazines *Lancio Story* and *Skorpio*.

After 1980 Serpieri worked on collections like *Découvrir la Bible* (*Discover the Bible*), as well as short stories for magazines such as *L'Eternauta*, *Il Fumetto*, and *Orient-Express*.

In 1985, Serpieri drew his most famous creation; the perfectly proportioned—and frequently naked—space siren, Druuna, in the science fiction epic *Morbus Gravis*. The intelligent and complex story of a plague-ridden city where humans degenerate into hideous mutations dealt with many complex themes, from sexual objectification of women, to the nature of what it means to be human. The book was an instant hit and the Italian public's demand for more of the voluptuous vixen was insatiable.

Below:
Serpieri's cover to the first book in his Druuna saga, 1985's *Morbus Gravis* (Severe Disease).

Right:
Druuna engages in fantasy sex on a beach with a desperately needy blond man.

Opposite page, right:
Druuna is ravaged by hideous mutations in *Morbus Gravis*.

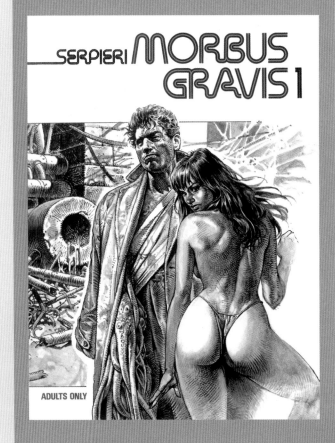

Over the years more Druuna sagas followed including, *Druuna* (1987), *Creatura* (1990), *Carnivora* (1992), *Mandragore* (1995), *Aphrodisia* (1997), and *Clone* (2003). As the series progressed, the erotic content increased with each volume until full, uncensored penetration shots were a regular feature. Serpieri even drew himself into the strip as the moustached character, Doc.

These erotic galactic epics sold over one million issues in 12 languages and Serpieri's fame spread in the English-speaking world, mostly thanks to translations of Druuna's adventures in *Heavy Metal* magazine.

Serpieri's intensely rendered artwork, lush, vivid colors — particularly the use of red — and fastidious depiction of the erotic anatomy of the well-endowed heroine has earned him the undisputed, and possibly slightly dubious, honorary title of the "Master of the Ass." This led to several sketchbooks of wanton goddesses and scenes of explicit congress, such as *Obsession, Druuna X, Druuna X 2, Croquis, Serpieri Sketchbook, Serpieri Sketchbook 2,* and *The Sweet Smell of Woman.*

But when the Druuna book, *The Forgotten Planet* (2000) failed to deliver the erotic goods, many fans were disappointed. But Serpieri made a very clear distinction between integral erotica and out and out porn: "I absolutely did not censor *The Forgotten Planet.* As it turned out, this story didn't need any erotic scenes. I do not draw erotic scenes to fill pages, they should be justified."

FRANCISCO SOLANO LÓPEZ

Although born in Argentina in 1928, it's really in Europe that Francisco Solano López made his name as a comic artist. His first published work, *Perico y Guillerma*, was in the early 1950s for Columbia, based in Buenos Aires.

He then joined Abril Editorial, where he illustrated several series written by the legendary Hector German Oesterheld, including the science-fiction series *El Eternauta*. López co-founded Frontera publishers with Oesterheld, and alternated on the Ernie Pike series with Hugo Pratt, Jorge Moliterni, and José Muñoz. López also worked on many British comics, including Fleetway's classic *Kelly's Eye* series. In fact, López received so much work from Fleetway that he opened his own art studio in Buenos Aires to complete the work, employing greats like Tibor Horvath, Julio and Jorge Schiaffino, and Nestor Morales to ink his penciled pages.

In 1976, while on a business trip to Spain, Lopez's house in Buenos Aries mysteriously burnt down and, suspecting the repressive military government, López moved his family to Madrid. Oesterheld and his daughters weren't so lucky, and were murdered by the fascist Junta as they were marked out as dissidents.

1984 found Lopez living in Rio de Janeiro where he began to produce work for the American market, working for such publishers as Dark Horse and Fantagraphics. He teamed up with fellow Argentine writer Ricardo Barreiro in the 1990s, working for the series *Las Aventuras de Lilian y Agatha* (*The Adventures of Lilian and Agatha*), better known in English as *The Young Witches* — a tale of magic, power, sex, and sadism. Set in England in the last third of the 19th century, it tells the story of the orphaned young Lilian Cunnington, sent to her aunt's, near Coventry. Lilian's relatives are the leaders of a coven of witches, "whose twisted rituals involve their nubile charges," and Lilian soon develops her latent powerful psychic abilities and omnisexual potential.

The Young Witches became one of the world's most popular, and certainly most reprinted, erotic comic series and this — along with his silent, full-color *Sexy Symphony* strip (produced with his son Gabriel Solano López) for Spain's *Kiss Comix* — ensured that López won the Best Erotic Author award at the Barcelona Erotic Salon.

Below:
A moving scene from López's political drama, *Ana*, as she recalls her dead lover.

Right:
The covers to Solano López's issues of *The Young Witches*.

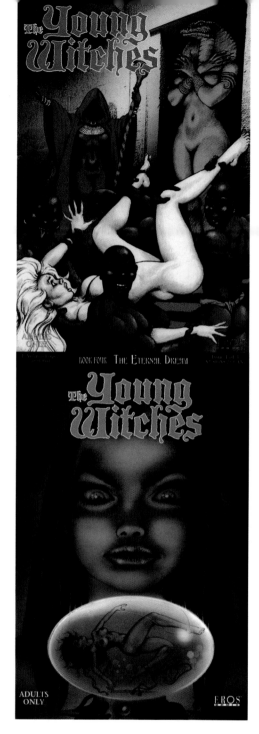

Opposite page, top:
One of Solano's near-silent *Sex Symphony* strips from Spain's *Kiss Comix*.

Opposite page, bottom:
Ana engages in sexual politics and manipulation in the Jean-Paul Sartre and Simone de Beauvoir inspired graphic novel written by Francisco Solano Lopez's son, Gabriel.

IGNACIO NOÉ

López's younger, fellow Argentine artist, Ignacio Noé, has taken erotica to a new level with his full-color stories. In a highly rendered style the artist works in mixed media — traditionally in acrylics — but more recently has moved to working completely digitally.

His work has subsequently appeared right across Europe in a multitude of erotic comic anthologies, including *Kiss Comix* in Spain (published by La Cúpula Editions), *Selen* magazine in Italy, and in the Dutch edition of *Penthouse Comix*.

His most notable erotic work is *Convent of Hell*, written by Solano López's collaborator Ricardo Barreiro, in 1995. This debauched masterpiece sees a Spanish convent full of repressed sexual desires, which are unleashed when the devil is inadvertently set free and reigns down an unholy bedlam of depravity and lust. Beautifully painted, the graphic novel was originally serialized in *Kiss*. It was published in America by NBM's Eurotica imprint, and they have since released many other books by the Argentine. After collaborating with Barreiro, Noé began writing as well as drawing, and his other collections of tongue-in-cheek short stories include *Doctor, I'm Too Big!*, *Ship of Fools*, and *The Piano Tuner*. The latter recounts the (mis) fortunes of the eponymous hero in a style reminiscent of the late 1970s British film sex comedies, *Confessions of a...* with their saucy humor and cheeky sexy situations, as the tuner finds himself *in flagrante* more times than is thought possible, making piano tuning one of the sexiest jobs ever.

Right:
Noé's Piano Tuner returns to the conservatory and discovers an unusual instrument.

Opposite page:
The digitally painted artwork of Ignacio Noe is simultaneously erotic and ridiculously silly, with over the top sound effects emphasising the latter.

GIOVANNA CASOTTO

One of the most popular Italian erotic artists working today is — perhaps surprisingly, in a genre dominated by male artists — a woman, Giovanna Casotto.

"I was just a housewife!" exclaimed Casotto, explaining how she got into the fumetti industry. "But when I started reading the comics my husband collected (*Comic Art*, *Orient-Express*, *Frigidaire*, and *Glamour International*), I started to get interested. Not so much for the erotic content, but by looking at the art because I have always had a passion for art. I liked to copy famous works by Rembrandt, Picasso, and so forth. I am especially interested in the naked human figure," the artist revealed in an interview with Vincenzo Raucci. "When I saw [the infamous bondage comic] *The Blonde* by Franco Saudelli

This page:
Casotto's photorealistic pencil studies are some of the best erotic artwork in comics today. Her clever use of limited color palette places emphasis on key aspects and intensifies the mood.

Opposite page, top left:
This voyeuristic strip, *Una playa solitaria* (*A solitary beach*) appeared in black and white in the Spanish erotic comic anthology *Kiss Comix* #163.

Opposite page, top right:
Casotto often used herself as the main model for her work, as seen here.

it was a revelation. I applied to the School of Comics in Milan with a copy of *The Blonde* in hand saying: 'I want to draw like this! I want to become like him!'" Casotto studied art for three years and was also inspired by fellow Italian erotic artist, Leone Frollo.

After a short stint on adventure comics for L'Intrepido, she met Italian publisher Stefano Trentini who signed her up, "But the only work available was as a background artist for football stories. I hated football!" However in 1994 the publisher launched a new erotic magazine, based on, and named after, adult movie actress, Selèn. This was Casotto's "big break," as she supplied stylish and sexy strips and covers for *Selèn* magazine. And she was in excellent

company, with big names like Tanino Liberatore, Milo Manara, Stefano Natali, Luca Tarlazzi, and Stefano Mazzotti also contributing.

Being a stunning-looking woman, as well as a talented writer/artist, Casotto drew herself as the central character in these outrageous erotic tales. Unsurprisingly, this combination saw her rocket to fame in her home country.

She was invited as a guest and co-host on numerous Italian tabloid TV shows such as *Maurizio Costanzo Show*, *Harem*, *Mixer*, *Second Evening*, *The Special Envoy*, and many others. However, Italian television is notoriously exploitative and Casotto soon found herself as a reluctant celebrity appearing in newspapers and besieged by fans. "I feel very uncomfortable

in front of the cameras, with an audience, having to respond to someone… The public expects a lot from you, and they're not always satisfied…each show was a mini martyrdom. They constantly attacked, accusing me of creating pornography…" she revealed to Gisela Scerman—one of Casotto's models—in an interview. "I didn't watch television for about five years: I hate everything that comes out from that box! I have a computer at home, but I don't even know how to turn it on, much to the frustration of my daughters! So I chose this form of communication [comics] to stay peacefully and quietly in my world…I'm not a misanthrope, but I do need to have my little space to dream…"

"The stories in my comics are not important, they're just an excuse to draw!" explained Giovanna Casotto, "The art tells the story... Just the nuances of pencil shading give the feeling of carnality!"

Casotto's work has been published all over Europe, and Eros Comix reprinted her strips as the *Bitch In Heat* series in America. In 1994 she met her artistic mentor, Saudelli, and began to pose for him, with the two starting to collaborate together both artistically and personally. Like many continental European women, Casotto draws her goddesses with unshaven armpits. "Underarm hair is as mysterious as that of the pussy. Who knows what it hides? Some sweat? Mmm...good..." joked the sassy artist.

Casotto's exquisitely drawn comics ooze sex appeal and her often humorous short stories, which feature surprise endings, have won her both male and female fans of intelligent erotica. "The eroticism that I — and other women — enjoy is inspired by the pin-ups of the 1950s. It may appear that the woman is just a sex object, and maybe she is, but the viewer needs to be aware it is also very ironic... Moreover, the eroticism, for me, is carnality — a sense of flesh and body...senses!"

With true Italian passion, Casotto believes that her "drawing is a need to communicate, an act of love, a reason for living. My drawings are the language that communicates feelings and emotions."

Censorship is something the drawing diva finds hard to fathom. "How can your sex drive — that is so vital to human beings' existence — be considered pornographic or obscene? The border between eroticism and pornography varies with an individual's own taste and decency. Who can say that this or that image is pornographic rather than erotic?...Of course, the risk is to confuse reality with fantasy, but the borders of the fantasy clearly remain on a two-dimensional sheet of paper... Meanwhile, I continue to draw comics — erotic or pornographic as they may be, it doesn't matter! The aim is to satisfactorily act out some fantasies and share my emotions."

Casotto has recently been moving into erotic photography, with bondage as a major theme, but hopefully she won't stay away from her drawing board for too long. "The eroticism draws me in, in all its forms, from art to writing... everything that I am concerned with exudes eroticism..."

Opposite page, right:
While most of Casotto's work is extremely candid, there is a strong, wry sense of humor throughout her work, often with the men being the butt of the joke, or twist ending. Here, the message of safe sex is instilled as the woman puts a condom on the man.

Below:
A bondage study, obviously inspired by Casotto's artistic mentor and fellow erotic comic artist, Franco Saudelli, who specializes in bondage comics like *The Blonde*.

Left:
This strip sees an artist having an illicit affair with his model. When the former dies before completing his work, Casotto manages to make an astutely amusing comment on modern art, when the model displays their bedsheets as the canvas.

GLAMOUR INTERNATIONAL

Throughout the 1980s there was one
publication that galvanized Italian erotic artists:
the over-sized *Glamour International* magazine.
The huge 12in × 12in periodical featured
wraparound covers by some of the biggest
names in erotic comics, including Vittorio
Giardino, Guido Crepax, Franco Saudelli, Milo
Manara, and Leone Frollo. But the magazine's
remit was broader than just Italian artists and
lived up to its title by featuring erotic work
by comic artists such as the UK's John Bolton
and the USA's Dave Stevens, Alex Toth, Frank
Frazetta, and Bill Ward. In October 1986 Stevens
was the first American illustrator to provide
a cover, which was, of course, based on his
eternal muse, Bettie Page. Each issue explored a
different theme from Brothels and Bordellos and
Crimes and Gals, to the dubious Black Women
and Jungle Girls, with relevant comic strips,
photographs, and articles from around the world.
The magazine also reprinted classic cheesecake
from the 1950s underground bondage
illustrations and showcased the latest work
by top erotic artists.

Background:
A beautiful nude study by
Jordi Bernet from *Glamour
International* magazine.

Left:
The full cover to *Glamour
International 2* by *Little Ego*
artist Vittorio Giardino.

Right:
Italian artist Tanino Libertore's
biting satire on the women's
sexually-aware magazine,
Cosmopolitan, where women
learn how to exploit men for
their own ends.

SPANISH SCENE: SEVENTIES COMICS

After the death of General Francisco Franco in 1975, and the demise of 36 years of repressive right-wing government, Spain revelled in its newfound freedoms of expression. Dizzy with this revolutionary breath of fresh air, comic creators started to experiment with erotic storylines in spades. The comics, crude in both content and artistically, were black and white and mass-produced on cheap pulp paper with a glossy fully-painted cover.

Publishers like Ediciones Zinco and Editorial Astri had lurid covers enticing readers to discover *Secretos de Mujer: Confesiones eroticas de la autora* (*Secrets of a Woman: Erotic Confessions of the Author*); Hard International's *Mas Penes Para La Estrella* (*Penises for the Superstar*) and *Sex Azafatas* (*Sex Stewardesses*). In many cases the artwork was little better than the US *Tijuana Bibles* that preceded them and, similarly, many artists didn't

sign their work, either because the publishers wouldn't let them for fear of prosecution, or just out of shame.

One of the better drawn strips, *Ulula: Ula se Hace Monja* (*Ula as a Nun*) appeared in *Hembras Peligrosas* (*Dangerous Females*) in 1985, and told the story of Ula, a woman whose vagina becomes cursed by the devil and kills anyone who touches it. Ultimately, she becomes a nun until her faith cures her, at which point she immediately drops her religion, and her underwear, and starts fucking the nearest man, just in time for the monk who helped her to catch them in flagrante.

The story is indicative of thousands that were being published at the time, but there were also good quality titles being published, such as *El Cuervo* (*The Crow* — not to be confused with James O'Barr's gothic fantasy), which mixed humorous short strips with heavily sex-laden

gags. In the early '90s, Josep M. Beá (AKA Pere Calsina) created the highly sexed strips *Perversion Sexual* and *Sexo Loco* for *El Cuervo*.

Another key Catalonian comic that was part of this liberated movement was the adult comedy anthology, *El Jueves*, launched in 1977. The weekly comic always had a political edge, but pushed the satire too far when the cartoonists Guillermo Torres and Manel Fontdevila were fined €3,000 ($4,438) each in November 2007 when they were found guilty of having "vilified the crown in the most gratuitous and unnecessary way," as the judge put it. Their crime? Depicting Crown Prince Felipe and his wife Letizia having sex with the caption, "Do you realize, if you get pregnant this will be the closest thing I've done to work in my whole life." It referred to the government's announcement that it would pay Spanish couples for each new baby they had. Police seized copies of that issue of *El Jueves* and there was a outcry about the suppression of free speech, and a fear of returning to the repressive Franco era.

Opposite page, top right:
The cover to *Ultra Hard* #4 published by Editorial Astri.

Opposite page, bottom left:
A recent and disturbing strip by top Spanish artist, Man (aka Manolo Carot), a regular contributor to *Kiss Comix*.

Above:
Ulula's cursed vagina is examined more than once in the strip, *Ula se Hace Monja*, from the anthology, *Hembras Peligrosas*.

Bottom center:
The below-par art from El Asistente's strip, *Las Cachondas Reclutas*, about two female volunteers' sexual adventures in the army.

Bottom right:
An unusual use for a kitchen utensil from the strip, *La Nieta Viciosa*, from *Ultra Hard* #4. Artist unknown.

SPANISH SCENE: *EL VIBORA* AND *KISS*

When the nascent Spanish underground comics movement got started, the flagship title that brought the creators together was *El Vibora*. Launched in 1979, the comics anthology has almost always featured a sexy, semi-clad woman on the cover. The title was the home of great Catalonian artists such as Max, whose earliest works included *Peter Pank*, a sexy punk version of Peter Pan.

El Vibora was at the cutting edge of the Spanish comics scene and reprinted US stars like Kevin Taylor and underground comix king Gilbert Shelton, as well as home-grown creators like Jaime Martín and the politically incorrect cartoonist Álvarez Rabo. As time went by the sexual content quota steadily increased until the majority of the magazine became devoted to sequential erotica.

El Vibora's publishers, La Cúpula, also published *Kiss Comix*, possibly one of the world's most renowned erotic comic anthologies. *Kiss #1* featured erotic cartoonist Kevin Taylor's *Girl* and work by Japanese mangaka, Chiyoji. Other contributors over the years have included Solano López and Noé, and Armas. In 1994, a sister publication was launched in France, which changed its name with issue 38 to *La Poudre Aux Rêves* (*The Stuff of Dreams*). Just to confuse matters even more, La Cúpula

then launched *French Kiss*, an English language edition of the magazine, in 2005. The publisher has published practically every single erotic sequential artist, either historically or working today in their *Coleccion X* series of graphic novels, including Frenchman Georges Levis, the British Erich Von Götha, Spaniard Luis Tobalina and the Chilean, Ferocius.

More recently Laura Perez Vernetti-Blina (better known as just Laura) a Barcelona-born writer, designer, and illustrator has created several erotic graphic novels. Her first, *Las Habitaciones Desmanteladas* (*The Dismantled Rooms*), was a series of short stories created in different styles, which she followed up with an erotic adaptation of *1001 Arabian Nights*, in 2002. Laura then teamed up with writer A. Altarriba in 2005 for *Amores Locos* (*Crazy Loves*) three stories of obsession and passion set in prehistory, Ancient Greece, and New York in the 1920s. Laura's stark and stylized black and white erotica has also seen her work published in Japan, by Kodasha.

Right:
The cover to *Kiss Comix* #163 drawn by Monica and Violeta.

Far Right:
Tobalina's Piketes strip from a 2005 edition of *Kiss Comix*.

Opposite page, top left:
R.E.M by Gabriel Bobillo put an erotic twist on the classic tale of *Jason and the Golden Fleece*, complete with a sex-starved Minotaur.

Opposite page, top right:
Miguel Angel Martin's strip *Anal Probe* (or *Girl Fuck Boy*) from Eros Comix's *Dirty Stories*.

Opposite page, bottom:
The animation cel-painting style of Atilio Gambedotti and Iván Guevara's *Akeronya* serial mixes traditional fantasy and superhero elements.

JORDI BERNET'S *CLARA DE NOCHE*

First appearing in 1992 in the pages of Spanish adult humor anthology, *El Jueves*, *Clara de Noche* (*Clara of the Night*) was an instant hit. The brainchild of artist Jordi Bernet, Clara was designed to be the classic "tart with a heart" — a working girl and single mother who was raising her son and dreaming of a better life. So far, so good. Realising that perhaps his writing wasn't up to the task of such a complex character, Bernet hired Argentine comics writers Carlos Trillo and Eduardo Maicas to handle the text chores.

Visually, Bernet based his character on the notorious 1950s model Bettie Page, a source of inspiration for many comic artists. When Eros Comix first translated the series into English, the title was changed to *Betty by the Hour*, acknowledging the model muse.

While Bernet's artwork looks simultaneously gorgeous (Clara) and goofy (her clients), Trillo's scripts unfortunately leave a bad misogynistic taste in the mouth. The constant references to Clara as a "whore;" the fact that all the married men sleep with her is dealt as a joke, and the tone of most of the two-page stories is embittered and nasty. Clara gives her son, Pablito, a kitten to keep him company while she works (she doesn't know that he knows she's a sex worker). But when the cat runs off to have sex with a Tom in the alley, Pablito's response is "Sheez!! All the women around here are alike! What a bitch!" Of course, all of this could be a misunderstanding as the scripts are written in an Argentine dialect, which needs translating into Spanish, and subsequently turned into English. In his defence, Bernet said, "This is a tribute to those ladies who work in what is said to be the oldest profession in the world, and we believe that if this profession has lasted this long, something about it has to be good and useful." An argument unlikely to wash with many feminists.

Clara has been collected into three albums in Spanish between 1993 and 1995, and the first album in English, a "best of," was published by Big Wow Art/Auad Publishing in 2006.

Background:
This more realistic rendering of Clara was created by Jordi Bernet for his "Black Series."

Above:
The cover to the English-language edition of *Clara of the Night*, published by Auad.

Right:
A typical *Clara* story, from the pages of *El Jueves*, has a bizarre twist, when a wife pays Clara to do a striptease for her TV obsessed husband to remind him what "real life" is all about. The strip continues the long-standing tradition of portraying men as goofball idiots who fall apart around sensuous women, who in turn, seem generally ambivalent about their paramours.

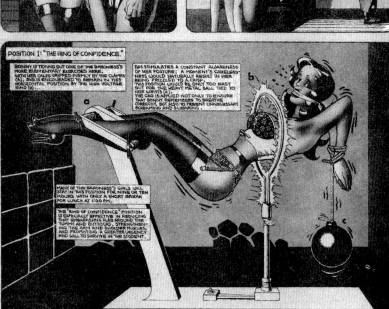

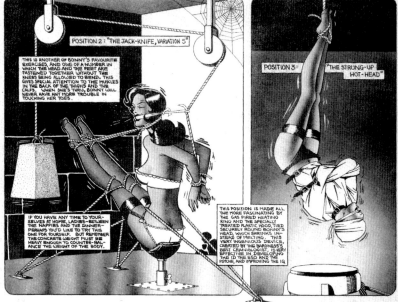

UK UNDERGROUND SEX COMICS: GRAPHIXUS AND ANTONIO GHURA

In the UK the situation has been a little less overt than their Continental cousins, but by no means less important in the development of comics in general, regardless of whether erotic or not. With a long history of bawdy and saucy comic illustrators, from Thomas Rowlandson and James Gilray to Aubrey Beardsley and Donald McGill, its hardly surprising that the UK would develop it's own underground comix scene. While not as large as the Californian scene, UK underground comix in the '70s were the seedbed for some of the greatest creators working in comics today, including Brian Bolland, Garry Leach, Dave Gibbons, John Higgins, and Bryan Talbot.

Robert Crumb's influence stretched all the way from the San Francisco comix communes to the UK, encouraging British creators to be more sexually daring in their work. One for the frontrunners of this rising movement was Antonio Ghura. Inspired by the American romance comics of the '50s, and their UK counterparts, Ghura created *Truly Amazing Love Stories* in 1977. The comic's cover featured a couple in a clinch, with the man exclaiming, "Oh Lord! I've just come in my pants!" Inside was the tale of the explicit seduction of young Jonathan by his Auntie Jean and, even more bizarrely, Bluebell the cow. Torn between the choice of incest and bestiality the man picks the former in this provocative, and farcical, parody. It was another six years before

Ghura released #2 of *Truly Amazing Love Stories*, yet the years had not diminished his zeal for sexual content. Inside were two graphic gay love stories, *Remember Rodney* and *I Lied for Love*, which were unflinching in their non-sensational portrayal of anal and oral sex, making them extremely cutting edge for the period. The comic also featured Batman and Robin as a pair of twisted rapists in a one-page strip, fulfilling Dr. Frederic Wertham's worst fears about superheroes.

But even Ghura managed to shock himself when he wrote and drew the strip *I Loved a Sex Fiend*, which attempted to make light of the Yorkshire Ripper case. After a sustained rape sequence, the attacker (Paul Rutcliffe, instead of real-life Peter Sutcliffe) is caught by the police and de-masked à la Scooby-Doo, with the weak caveat "Rape is no fun at all!" "I wanted to be outrageous," the writer/artist remorsefully explained in *Headpress* #18. "Most people didn't like it...Looking back at it, maybe I should have left it out."

In 1978 Mal Burns produced the comic magazine anthology, *Graphixus*. It featured Brian Bolland, who paid homage to Winsor McCay with his sexual adventures of *Little Nympho in Slumberland*—just as Vittorio Giardino would 11 years later in Italy (Bolland's strip was originally drawn in 1973). *Little Nympho in Slumberland* managed to alienate feminists and readers when the central protagonist appeared naked on the cover to #3. By today's standards it looks pretty tame, but it certainly provoked many to write in and complain.

In the following issue of *Graphixus* (#4), Bolland also paid his dues to bondage artist supreme, John Willie, with his *The Bizarre Weight Watchers' Guide*. The strip parodied Willie's complex bondage art, with women tied to Heath Robinson-esque machines like "The Filly Sucker" with the pretence of losing weight. With such edgy material appearing in the underground comix, it was only a matter of time before the authorities started to take notice.

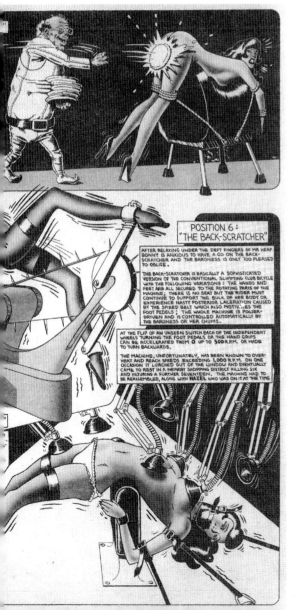

Opposite page, top left:
John Higgins's art for the Zirk strip, *Marooned*, written by Pedro Henry (aka Steve Moore) that appeared in the *Heavy Metal War Machine* special in 1993. Higgins, like many British artists, got his first breaks in the UK fanzine and underground scene.

Top Left:
Garry Leach's cover to *Graphixus* #2, featuring his "erotik space fantasy" *Succuba*.

Opposite page, bottom:
Brian Bolland's pastiche/homage to John Willie's classic *Bizarre* magazine. The strip appeared in *Graphixus* #4, and Bolland is clearly aping Willie's elongated art style. Curiously, that issue's editorial stated that there was no sexual content inside. Bolland eventually drew mainstream superhero comics for US publishers like DC Comics.

UK UNDERGROUND SEX COMICS:
THE NASTY TALES TRIAL

Just like their compatriots in the United States, Britain's comic creators and publishers faced censorship, but mostly for reprinting US creators such as Robert Crumb and Gilbert Shelton.

The *IT (International Times)* was an alternative newspaper and a voice of counterculture alongside the renowned *Oz* magazine. *Oz*'s editors, Richard Neville, Jim Anderson, and Felix Dennis were charged with obscenity in 1971 with their infamous "School Kids Issue." The art that got them into trouble was a collage created by 15-year-old schoolboy, Vivian Berger, which merged a children's Rupert the Bear annual with Crumb's sexually explicit comic strip, *Eggs Ackley in the Land of the Vulture Demonesses*, from Big Ass Comics. All three editors were found guilty and sentenced to 15 months in prison. However, their custodial sentences were overturned on appeal.

Meanwhile, *IT* helped finance a new comics anthology, *Nasty Tales*, in 1971, which featured the work of UK creators Edward Barker, Chris Welch, and others. In 1973 the offices were raided, all 275 copies of *Nasty Tales* #1 were seized and Paul Lewis, Edward Barker, and Mick and Joy Farren, were brought before

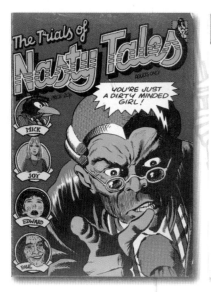

Left:
The covers to *The Trials of Nasty Tales* (cover by Dave Gibbons); #7 with the warning: "Strong stomached adults only;" and #5, which reprinted Greg Irons' classic anti-Vietnam war strip, *The Legion of Charlies*.

Background:
Chris Welch's cult character, Ogoth, faces a similar fate to *Trashman* on the opposite page in *Nasty Tales* #3.

the courts on charges of obscenity. The nine-day trial was farcical in places, with Barker's drink/drug-addled, mumbling, semi-coherent testimony, and Joy's bursting into tears, doing more harm than good. The defence argued that their reprinting of Crumb's *Grand Opening of the Great Intercontinental Fuck-in and Orgy Riot* cartoon was as a piece of important satire with famous writers like George Perry and Germaine Greer defending the cartoonist's work. "Of all underground cartoonists I think Crumb is the best...Among comic strips and comic books this is rather better than most and a good deal less insidious in its effect upon public taste than Superman," explained outspoken feminist Greer. Judge Alan King-Hamilton declared in his summing up, "You may be surprised that anybody came forward to tell you that anything in this magazine has literary or artistic merit. But there you are. This world is full of surprises and it happened." The defendants got another surprise when, amazingly, the entire *Nasty Tales* team were let off with a caution — although the reasons are spurious to say the least (one juror wanted to go home and another just thought the comic was "rubbish").

The whole trial was summarized in the special edition, *The Trials of Nasty Tales*, with transcripts drawn by Dave Gibbons, and others. But the trial effectively killed the title dead, and with huge court fees to pay, and sales in general declining, *Nasty Tales* only lasted 7 issues.

But this wouldn't be the last time that Robert Crumb's artwork would be in the dock. Twenty-three years later, Knockabout Comics would have to go through exactly the same arguments all over again.

Left:
Spain Rodriguez's *Trashman* was reprinted in the UK's *Nasty Tales*. Here the artist turns the sexual tables on his eponymous hero by having him sexually used by neo-feminists.

UK SCENE: KNOCKABOUT VS. CUSTOMS

The biggest and most successful underground publisher to emerge from the UK in the '70s was Knockabout Comics. It was set up by Tony and Carol Bennett after the demise of the former's combined publishing house, distribution network, and commune, Unicorn, in 1975. It began by publishing Gilbert Shelton's *Fabulous Furry Freak Brothers* which helped clear Bennett's debts.

As they expanded their range of titles, they included the work of Hunt Emerson and Mike Matthews, as well as many other leading artists. "At Knockabout, our books are only sold to adults, or if younger people read them they are likely to be growing up twisted anyhow," explained Tony Bennett, somewhat cavalierly.

In July, 1982 the Obscene Publications Squad seized 75 titles, including *Dope Comix*, *Cocaine Comix*, and Antonio Ghura's *Amazing Love Stories*. In May, 1983 Knockabout endured a long trial at the Central Criminal Court (The Old Bailey) in London under the Obscene

Publications Act, as to whether drug references in comics should be allowed, and whether such references would "corrupt and deprave." They were acquitted on all charges and this enabled a certain liberalization of comics, cannabis-related books, and the UK's shops selling such material. But the court case took its toll on Knockabout for years and it wasn't "worth it financially, or for all the worry and hassle, but certainly I would do it again if I had to," said a defiant Tony Bennett.

In order to recoup their court costs of nearly £7,000, the publishers released the *Bumper Knockabout Trial Special* hardcover in 1984, featuring donated work by Alan Moore, Hunt Emerson, political newspaper cartoonist Steve Bell, Bryan Talbot, and Melinda Gebbie.

But the authorities weren't going to let the maverick publisher off so easily and they didn't like losing. They saw their chance for revenge in 1996 when the British Customs and Excise department seized Knockabout's imports

of Robert Crumb's *My Trouble with Women* collection. Despite having a previous 1988 letter from Customs stating that Knockabout could import the book, Tony Bennett had to defend the seemingly incongruous (to the Government) mix of comics and explicit sexual imagery to the courts. "There is certainly a perception in Britain and the rest of the English-speaking world that comics are for kids...Comics may be ephemeral and 'low art' but every newspaper carries comic strips, many of which are aimed solely at an adult readership, although I suspect that quite a lot of those adult readers might be shocked at what is inside the covers of many modern comic books," Bennett mused 10 years after the case.

Fellow publisher, comics historian, and author, Paul Gravett, was called in as a character witness for the defense — explaining how Crumb was simply following in the long tradition of Thomas Rowlandson and James Gilray. Andrew Bird, who represented Customs and Excise,

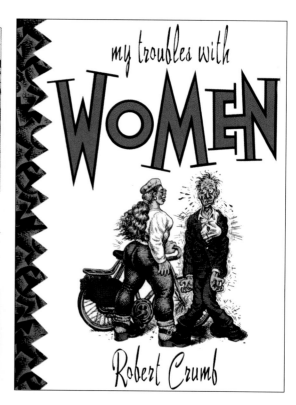

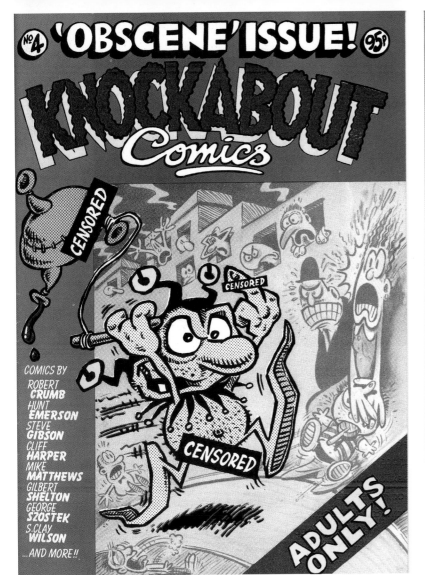

bizarrely stated, "The artistic merit of these items is wholly irrelevant to deciding whether they are obscene." Tony Bennett recalled, "We won this overwhelmingly...and Customs were kind enough to write to me after the case setting out a list of what sex acts might be shown in comics. I haven't actually framed it, but it is a precious document." The courts awarded legal costs of £6,000 to Knockabout, and their defense lawyer, Geoffrey Robertson, declared: "This customs decision would have put at risk all the underground art of the '60s and we were very happy to put a stop to any such trend."

"The agencies of the government that deal with censorship use a somewhat heavy-handed economic weapon by seizing goods and then taking a long time to bring them to trial, and even when the defendant is acquitted there is no compensation for loss of business. Before our big trial in the '80s the police had many of our books for nearly three years," said Bennett.

However, the cases did push the issue of censorship to the fore, particularly in relation to sequential art and Bennett concedes, "Censorship is not nearly so bad [these days] partly due to the successful results of some of our own battles with HM Customs and the Obscene Publications Branch...Without intending to, at the time we helped to change the law, or at least the way the law is used."

HUNT EMERSON

Britain's less perverted answer to Robert Crumb was the equally talented Hunt Emerson, who was born in Newcastle in 1952. After moving to the UK's second-largest city, Birmingham, to study at the Art College he co-founded the Birmingham Arts Lab's comics division in 1972. Their first publication was *Large Cow Comix*, featuring mostly work by Emerson. The artist was inspired by underground comics by Gilbert Shelton, Crumb, and the like, which he bought from Carol Bennett, who was running a "head shop" in Birmingham at the time.

Emerson adapted D.H. Lawrence's infamous erotic novel *Lady Chatterley's Lover* in 1986, 26 years after the obscenity trial that finally saw the book published legally in the UK. The cover of Emerson's graphic novel even warned "Not for sale to wives or servants," a dig at the failed — and justly ridiculed — chief prosecutor, Mervyn Griffith-Jones, who asked in court if it were the kind of book "you would wish your wife or servants to read." In typical Emerson style, he tempers the lusty ruttings of Mellors, the gamekeeper, and Lady Chatterley with sight gags and comedic moments.

Emerson's next foray into the world of erotica was his 1993 adaptation of *Casanova's Last Stand*. Featuring the aging lothario, this fast and loose adaptation of the writer's autobiography is simultaneously sexy and silly, and as Casanova wrote in 1791, "I am writing my life to laugh at myself, and I am succeeding." He would have surely approved of Emerson's take on his work. The graphic novel was feted by critics and it appears on the French National Library's website. But despite its critical success, *Casanova's Last Stand* only sold about half of its initial 5,000-copy print run in 14 years, according to Emerson.

In 2000, Emerson was named as one of the 75 European Masters of Cartooning of the 20th Century by the Centre Nationale de la Bande Dessinee et de l'Image, (CNBDI) in Angouleme, France.

Emerson continued adapting great literary classics, such as Coleridge's *Rime of the Ancient Mariner* and most recently Dante's *Inferno*, but his contribution to erotic sequential art didn't finish with just two graphic novels.

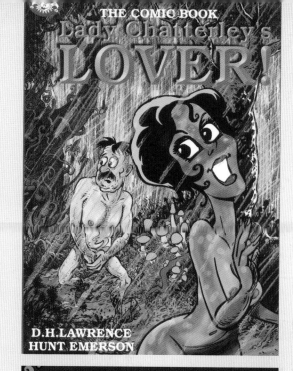

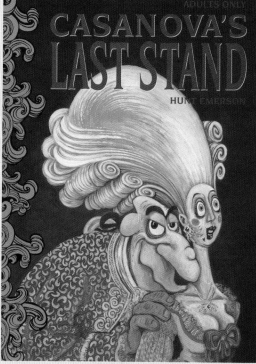

Bottom left:
A tender moment between Mellors and Lady Chatterley.

Top right:
Hunt Emerson's cover to his 1986 adaptation of *Lady Chatterley's Lover*.

Center right:
The cover to the *Casanova's Last Stand* graphic novel.

Opposite page, left:
Several scenes from *Lady Chatterley's Lover* revealing a candid, yet romantic story. As two fish comment, "A filthy sexual act!" "Nope—a great work of literature."

Opposite page, right:
Emerson cleverly uses visual symbolism to indicate Lady Chatterley's orgasm, and reveals his underground comix roots in the process.

BRITISH MEN'S MAGAZINES: *MEN ONLY*, *FIESTA*, AND *FIRKIN THE CAT*

Emerson teamed up with writer Tym Manley in 1981 for their strip *Firkin the Cat*, which was created for the top-shelf men's magazine, *Fiesta*. Manley was a regular contributor to men's magazines, writing for *Club* as far back as January, 1980. *Firkin* was indicative of how many British creators viewed erotic comics, full of goofy gags and observations on the ludicrousness of humans in their eternal pursuit to get their rocks off. Firkin acted as an observer and commentator on the endless bizarre sexual peccadilloes that Manley and Emerson shone their satirical spotlight on. "We like to point out to people that all the Firkin stories are closely based on personal research," joked the cartoonist. "The Firkin comics are a debunking view of the sex industries, if they're anything, but hey, they're only bloody comic strips after all!"

"When I first started doing Firkin I used to get trouble from some of my women friends, but that was at a time when feminism was very militant anyway," said Emerson in an interview in 2007. "These days nobody cares very much. Most people I know don't see my work at all, whether it's *Fiesta* work or any other. In a world where erotic magazines exist, *Fiesta* is one of the less virulent ones."

Apart from *Firkin*, British men's magazines haven't had quite the eminent illustrations as their US cousins, such as *Playboy* and *Penthouse* — although the latter did run *O, Wicked Wanda* by Frederic Mullally and Ron Embleton in the UK edition. In 2006 *Men Only* magazine started running *Brit Starr*, a blonde wannabe-starlet who will have sex with anyone or anything to get those column inches or her face on the news. Written by John A. Short and drawn by Gabrielle Noble, the monthly strip is a satire on society's celebrity-obsessed culture, where fame is the only thing that counts, even if it costs you your dignity. Short and Noble had previously contributed to Eros Comix numerous specialty sex anthologies, including *Head* (cunnilingus), *Rear Entry* (anal sex), *Dildo* (sex toys), and *Pee Soup* (watersports), and *Brit Starr* continues the tradition of blatantly pornographic comics.

Editor's Note: THE GRAFENBURG—OR "G"—SPOT IS A THICKENING OF THE VAGINA ROUGHLY ON A LEVEL WITH THE PUBIC BONE. STIMULATION PRODUCES ORGASMS SO INTENSE SHE'LL PEE ALL OVER YOU. LOVELY—THANK YOU, MR. EDITOR.

Opposite page:
Bearded writer Tym Manley and bespectled artist Hunt Emerson guest star in their own *Firkin the Cat* strip.

Above:
Firkin the Cat's constant dismay at human's sexual antics has appeared in *Fiesta* for over 27 years.

Right:
John A. Short and Gabrielle Noble's *Brit Starr* from the pages of *Men Only*—the men's top shelf magazine.

LYNN PAULA RUSSELL

One of the UK's lesser-known, but equally important, erotic sequential artists is Lynn Paula Russell. No stranger to the adult entertainment business, Russell had a successful career as an adult movie actress in the '70s/'80s under the nom de sexe, Paula Meadows. She went on to edit *Fessée*, a British spanking/corporal punishment (CP) magazine, published by Janus. Russell's first professional illustration work was when she was 27, drawing a children's book, *Beyond the Midnight Mountains*, written by her husband, Frank Charles. She also painted portraits of fellow West End theater actors and other personalities.

While many of her illustrations graced the pages and covers of *Fessée*, it wasn't until 1990 when she drew her first sequential strip. "Fellow erotic artist Erich von Götha put me in touch with a publisher in Paris who set me going on strip cartoons. I was completely new to it and had to evolve my own way of telling a story. Aided by my writer husband, I decided to use my

own experiences as a starting point to construct a story line set in the 1920s," explained a candid Russell. "It was called *Sophisticated Ladies*. Obviously the situations were different from those in my real life, but the central character reflected my own wonderment and sense of adventure as I set out on a voyage of discovery into the S&M world, back in my early thirties."

"Storytelling with pictures and dialog really appealed to me because it brought together my two chief interests — theater and erotic scenarios....However, I remain predominantly an illustrator because I am unable to use artistic shorthand to swiftly produce the graphic effects I want."

An unabashed and highly visible member of the BDSM (Bondage, Disciple, Sadomasochism) community, Russell has incorporated her experiences into her comics, "How else would I be able to picture all these activities? All of it is done from my memories and imagination, but the main characters in *Summer Holiday* and *Sophisticated Ladies* do tend to resemble my younger, more innocent self. I don't seem to be able to help that. Having been rather an exhibitionist in my younger days and enjoyed treading the boards, it is obvious that I would give myself the best roles in my own scenarios!"

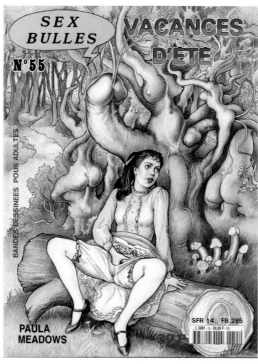

Top left:
A photo-realistic illustration by Lynn Paula Russell rendered in color pencil for *Fessée* magazine.

Left:
The cover to the French erotic magazine, *Sex Bulles* #55, which was a Russell special with the story, *Vacances d'été*. Note on the cover the hidden phallic symbols and erotic imagery, and that the artist was using her previous pen name, Paula Meadows.

Opposite page, left:
A page from *Sophisticated Ladies*, Russell's 1920's fantasy in which the artist placed herself as the central protagonist, seen here in the last three panels.

Opposite page, top right:
A ménage a tois from *Vacances d'été*, drawn in pen and ink, a rarely used medium by Russell.

Opposite page, bottom right:
An extreme S&M fantasy illustration. Note the phallic pattern on the floor, which holds the composition together.

Above, left:
The color–penciled—with pen and ink—cover to *Sabina* (2006) drawn by Lynn Paula Russell

Left:
An exquisitely rendered spanking illustration from *Fessée* magazine, created in color pencils by Meadows.

Above:
A lesbian tryst between Sabina and her friend, Mandy. Like most erotic graphic novels, Sabine has few, if any, serious repercussions from all the promiscuity.

Lynn Paula Russell works in multiple media, including colored pencils and water colors, but "my favourite technique is pencil and ink...To do color work using pencils would not be practical for strip cartoons, so I have always stuck to black and white, which I really like. Now that computer programs exist that can facilitate this kind of art I might start to use color in the future."

Russell's work has covered paintings inspired by erotic classics like *The Story of O* and the *Kama Sutra*, as well as the two graphic novels, *SABINA* 1 and 2. The latter recounts the sexual adventures of Sabina, a high-class courtesan who goes from the "rough trade" of London's most sordid slums to the crème de la crème of British society. "Sabina, aka Sabine, is the creation of [the anonymous] French writer ["A.P."] and she is much more glamorous and predatory than I could ever be," said the artist, whose work is published by The Erotic Print Society in the UK.

By Russell's own admission, she found the initial transition to sequential art a laborious act of love. "I suppose it took me about a fortnight to finish my monthly contribution of five or six pages, but sometimes longer. One can start to work into a favorite drawing, adding details and tones. Sometimes it is difficult to stop!"

Russell's artistic influences draw from wide and varied sources "In the erotic genre I admire Serpieri for the sheer power of his drawing and Loic Dubigeon for the way he handles tone." Her admiration for her friend and creative mentor, Erich von Götha, is for his "flowing movement and drama, the way he handles group scenes with such consummate ease or focuses on the intensity of a descending whip!" Other influences include fellow Europeans Alex Varenne, Milo Manara, and Georges Pichard. But Russell remains pragmatic: "Mainly I just do my own thing and try to achieve realism, feeling, and animation. Without emotional feeling, erotic art becomes static and dead. Sex is a dance that must be choreographed and lit like a piece of theater."

Above:
A page from Meadows' *Sabina*, showing the eponymous heroine as a carefree, sexual libertine.

ALAN MOORE, MELINDA GEBBIE, AND LOST GIRLS

Alan Moore is one of Britain's, if not the world's, pre-eminent comic scribes. Having revolutionized the superhero genre with his and Dave Gibbons' opus, *Watchmen*, Moore turned his attentions to erotic—or as he'd prefer to call them, pornographic — comics.

The starting point — revealed Moore to the Preston Speculative Fiction Group in a talk in 1993 — was the question: "Is there a way of doing pornography that is sexually arousing, is not offensive politically, aesthetically, or in all those other ways, that can speak to women as well as men, that can have characters, meaning, and a story the same way as ordinary literature?"

Moore wrestled with these huge themes, but it "didn't really come together until I met with Melinda Gebbie, a long time underground Californian artist."

San Francisco-born Gebbie discovered the comics in 1973 when she met writer/artist Lee Marrs at a publishers' fair. Formerly a fine artist, Gebbie contributed her first strip to *Wimmen's Comix #4*, the seminal all-women anthology published by Last Gasp. She then contributed to numerous anthologies, including *Tits & Clits*, *Wet Satin*, and *Anarchy*, and in 1977 she wrote and drew her solo title, *Fresca Zizis*.

In 1984 Gebbie moved to England to work on the animated adaptation of Raymond Briggs' anti-war graphic novel *When the Wind Blows*, while continuing to create strips for UK anthologies like *Strip AIDS* and *Heartbreak Hotel*. It was through her involvement with these publications that she got to know Alan Moore.

Possibly one of the most important erotic comics of the last 20 years, the plot of

Lost Girls evolves around three women, Wendy Darling, from *Peter Pan*; Dorothy Gale, from the *Wizard of Oz*; and Alice Fairchild, from *Alice in Wonderland*. All three meet in a hotel in Austria in 1913, on the cusp of World War I. Each one relates their sexual history via the erotic decoding of the classic stories.

Highly explicit, and beautifully drawn in pastels, the first six chapters of *Lost Girls* were initially published between 1991 and 1992 in the anthology *Taboo* starting in #5. Kitchen Sink Press' Tundra imprint later reprinted the *Taboo* chapters as two separate volumes, and a 10-issue series was planned. But Moore and Gebbie felt it was better to complete the project first before starting to republish it. Eventually, Top Shelf launched the trilogy at the July 2006 San Diego Comic-Con. The three volumes were

Right:
Melinda Gebbie's 1979 self-portrait alongside fellow underground comix artist, S. Clay Wilson. In the background are her interpretations of his comic strips.

Far right and Opposite page, bottom left:
A few of Gebbie's pages from *Lost Girls* Book Two, Chapter 12: Shaking and Waking, that pay homage to late 19th Century erotic painter Alphonse Mucha.

Opposite page, far right:
The cover to *Lost Girls* Book One drawn by Melinda Gebbie.

gathered into one slipcase edition and named after quotes from each classic book—*Volume1: Older Children* (*Alice in Wonderland*)*; Volume 2: Neverlands* (*Peter Pan*)*; Volume 3: The Great And Terrible* (*The Wizard of Oz*). The opus wasn't available in the UK until January 2008 because of issues with the copyright owners of *Peter Pan*, Great Ormond Street Hospital. Their copyright expired then, freeing Top Shelf to release it in the UK.

While working on the project, Moore and Gebbie became romantically involved and announced their engagement in 2005. "I'd recommend to anybody working on their relationship that they should try embarking on a 16-year elaborate pornography project together," joked the hirsute writer. "I think they'll find it works wonders." They eventually married in May 2007.

Right:
Gebbie's erotic interpretation of The Mad Hatter's tea party from *Alice in Wonderland*. This fantastical orgy appeared in Book 2 of *Lost Girls*.

Opposite page, top left:
Alan Moore's clever script reinterpreted classic children's literature and examined the sexual subtexts, in this case *Peter Pan*, with Wendy, being disturbed by a perverted "Captain Hook."

Opposite page, top right:
Dorothy, from *The Wizard of Oz*, recounts her early sexual awakenings in Kansas, in the allegorical tale of *The Straw Man* in Book 2.

Lost Girls was a commercial success, selling over 35,000 copies in first year, despite a $75 price tag—as well as a critical one. Novelist Michael Faber, in the UK's *Guardian* newspaper called *Lost Girls* "a humane and seductive defence of the inviolable right to dream," or as Brian Eno called it, an "Epoch-making — or at least 'epoch-shaking' — piece of work."

However, the book did come under criticism for potentially portraying child pornography—as the story recounts the sexual awaking of the three young, potentially underage, women—and many retailers stated that they wouldn't stock the book for fear of possible prosecution. In the United States, child pornography requires the involvement of a child in its production to be deemed obscene, which the book obviously did not include. The legality of the book in other countries—where some forbid any images of nude children in a sexual context, regardless of how they were produced—caused French publisher Delcourt to temporarily suspend their French edition.

Gebbie was no stranger to controversy as she was briefly involved in an obscenity trial when Knockabout comics were prosecuted by The UK's HM Customs and Excise for importing *Fresca Zizis* ("fresh cocks" in Italian). According to Gebbie, "The judge made me stand up in court and defend my work. There was objection to some of the autobiographical things in my stuff. I said, 'These things happened to me, and I wrote about them...so if you're going to find them obscene, you have to find the people whom I'm writing about obscene. I'm just writing about my life; I'm not trying to titillate anybody...' His verdict was that all the comics should be confiscated and burned. They burned all 400 copies of my comic and made them illegal in England to possess."

Moore has defended their work as a direct backlash against the "cold, dead-eyed" pornography that is mass-produced by the adult magazine and film industry. "A work of pornography generally leads to isolation, selfish lust, and unbearable loneliness. Once the object of the pornography has been achieved, then you can writhe in the sordid and degraded kind of loneliness of your abject existence. That's not the kind of feeling that I prefer to associate with sex," explained the Northampton writer.

"And yet, I think an awful lot of the millions of people who make use of pornography across the world must be regularly plunged into that very unpleasant kind of selfish space. There's no need for that. If pornography could be an aesthetic experience, an intellectual experience, and still be sexy, then it could be an incredibly useful tool that could heal a lot of people in areas where they have problems that they don't even know how to talk about or define. If pornography was used correctly, it could give a kind of forum for discussing sexual ideas."

4

Tits and Tentacles:
The Japanese Experience

CONFUSED CENSORSHIP AND PENAL CODES

When it comes to illustrated erotica, Japan has always stood out from the global crowd. Ever since the earliest erotic shunga prints of the 18th and 19th Centuries — a pornographic subgenre of the better known *ukiyo-e* (floating world) prints — Japanese culture has readily embraced extremely graphic sexual depictions. Shunga artists like Yanagawa Shigenobu and Miyagawa Isshô painted various couples, Geishas, and homosexual Samurai and their Kabuki "kagema" boyfriends *in flagrante*, and everyone from housewives and Samurai collected the ubiquitous graphic sex shunga.

This openness and acceptance has always sat uneasily with a more puritanical west, which prefers its sex behind closed doors and in brown paper bags. Because of this difference in approaches a lot of misnomers about Japanese culture have sprung up, particularly in relation to its sexual mores.

In the 1920s, a modernized, decadent Japanese society was captured by Saseo Ono, who drew erotic cartoons of the new, sexually liberated "flapper" girls. His images were regarded as *ero-guro-nansensu* (erotic-grotesque-nonsensical) art, a precursor to modern manga (comics).

Groundbreaking creators like Go Nagai —who would later invent the giant robot/ mecha genre with *Mazinger Z*—launched his *Harenchi Gakuen* (Shameless School) strip in the boy's comic, *Shonen Jump* in 1968. It featured extensive nudity, drinking, and mah jong games in a kid's comic. Naturally the PTAs across Japan

were up in arms, but it was the beginning of the modern erotic manga that would explode in the mid-1970s.

Over the years, Japanese manga developed and gradually drifted into clearly defined markets, generally broken down into five main categories: *shonen* (boys), *shojo* (girls), *redisu* or *redikomi* (ladies), *seijin* (adult erotica) and *seinen* (young men, which actually refers to 14–40-year-olds). Typically, these comics got separated down into almost infinite subdivisions, with seijin split into *futanari* (transexual), *lolicon* (Lolita complex), and many others. Despite the vast variety of weekly, monthly, and quarterly manga, these anthologies are ephemera, read quickly and thrown away. Japanese readers tend to keep the collected works of their favorite strips from the weeklies. These *bunkobon* (400-page collections) and *tankōbon* (200 page) are smaller and easier to store than their brick-sized progenitors.

Japan's sexual laws have always been a matter of contention both inside and outside the country. The age of consent is a surprisingly young 13, as specified by the Japanese Penal Code Articles 176 and 177, but positively, there are no sodomy laws, so homosexuality was never made illegal. However, most prefectures have ordinances that prohibit "immoral sexual acts with minors," an ambiguous phrase at the best of times. It is unclear if the translated term "minors" refers to children under 18 or to those who have not reached maturity—over 20, in Japanese law. Unbelievably, child pornography wasn't outlawed until 1999, after intense public lobbying. Probably the most important legal statute, in relation to erotic manga, is Article 175 of the vaguely worded Japanese Penal Code. This prevents the depiction of explicit sexual intercourse and adult genitalia in comics. Thus, no clear shots of penises, vaginas, or public hair are allowed to be depicted. It was this last point that prevents many shunga from being publicly displayed in galleries and would cause much consternation in the future.

HENTAI

The 1970s saw an explosion of erotic manga, and creators like Takashi Ishii became cult heroes. "My work wasn't porn," said the artist-turned-film-director in 1994. "It was about male-female relationships and communication... To depict this I had to use sex, because sex is a mirror of modern relations."

These relations soon picked up the moniker "hentai." In the West the term has become synonymous with overtly sexual manga and anime, but it actually has several meanings in Japan, including "metamorphosis" or "abnormality," but mostly it has the stronger negative implication, "sexually perverted" and explicit manga is more usually referred to as *jū hachi kin* ("prohibited for sale to persons under 18"). *Ecchi* manga — more akin to cheesecake pin-up art — also began appearing. Hentai anime and manga allow elements of sexual fantasy to be represented in ways that would be physically impossible or socially unacceptable in photography or live action film. As various specialized fetish comics developed, ludicrously exaggerated "Engrish" titles like *Women Live for Sacrificial Ripe Love!* and *Perverted Flight of Love* drew readers in. At their height, it was estimated that there were approximately 70-100 erotic manga titles available on the newsstand every month.

As in the West, manga has always had to deal with its detractors and issues with censorship, however lax that may appear to Western standards. Unfortunately, as publishers tried to circumnavigate Penal Code 175 they ended up causing more problems than they solved. Just because it was against the law to represent genitalia didn't stop creators from drawing them and publishers were forced to conceal the offending organs. Apocryphal tales of schoolgirls earning pocket money during their vacations by working for publishers, whiting out offending penises, vaginas, and pubic hair, soon appeared, making the whole censorship issue appear pointless. As time went by, publishers came up with increasingly inventive ways of covering sex organs, by using representational visuals, such as egg plants and rockets, and pixelation techniques. But these soon reduced in size to become a tiny black bar across a penis or a vague blurring of artwork to the point that it was just paying lip service to the law.

The loopholes around adult genitalia also led to the unfortunate rise of lolicon (Lolita complex) comics. Soon the whole uncomfortable image of sexy schoolgirls would have a firm grip on Japan's manhood.

Top right:
The appropriately nicknamed Kondom (aka Teruo Kakuta) writes and draws the incredibly popular *Bondage Fairies* series. Here the bi-sexual nymphs, Pamila and Pfil, are victims to sexual predator and bad fairy, Urushira.

Bottom right:
Masamune Shirow is a huge star, both in Japan and the west. He has often incorporated mild "cheesecake" pin-up in his more mainstream work, as well as drawing more explicit scenes.

Opposite page, top left:
Another sequence from Chiyoji's *Miss 130*, the story of a "working girl." Note, her large breasts could almost be serving this specific fetish, and the artist has indeed drawn bakunyu stories, including *Miss DD*.

Opposite page, top right:
Junko Mizuno's cute heroines having sex have a certain charm, but "Some people seem to find it more shocking. To them, it looks like I'm trying to dirty innocents."

Opposite page, bottom left:
Secret schoolgirl lesbian trysts are very popular in Japanese hentai, such as this scene from *Misty Girl Extreme* by Toshiki Yui, creator of *Hot Tails*.

Opposite page, bottom right:
This sequence from *Immoral Angel* by Koh Kawarajima first appeared in Japan in 1997 and was published in the west by CPM Manga in 2000.

LOLICON

The *kawaii* aesthetic ("cute") is extremely popular in Japan, particularly in manga. "Super-deformed" or "Chibi" versions of classic characters are regularly seen, and the ubiquitous *Hello Kitty* belongs to this ideology. Equally, the uniformed schoolgirl has also become a highly erotic and fetishist symbol in Japan—just as Britney Spears videos and *St. Trinian's* movies have in the West—only more so. These two concepts are so deeply ingrained into the Japanese psyche that, together, they create a strange collusion between the hentai and the kawaii, an eroticised ideal of anything cute.

When manga publishers realized they couldn't portray adult genitalia, they encouraged creators to draw younger-looking cute characters, as there was no law preventing the depiction of children's genitalia, an unfortunate loophole.

This genre of manga, lolicon, is perhaps the least defendable and most unpalatable to Western eyes. Also known as Lolicon or "Lolita complex" (after Vladimir Nabokov's book, *Lolita*, in which an older man becomes sexually obsessed with a 12-year-old girl) it is a widespread phenomenon in Japan, where it is a frequently criticized, yet many general bookstores and newsstands openly offer lolicon manga.

Throughout the 1980s, notable lolicon mangaka included Nonki Miyasu, Kamui Fujiwara, Yoshito Asari, and Aki Uchida. Hideo Azuma's 12-page story *The Machine That Came from the Sea* (*Umi Kara Kita Kikai*) was a good example of a self-published (doujinshi) sexual manga featuring young girls — as was Azuma's magazine *Cybele*. His work became popular among schoolboys because most of the erotic manga up until then had featured mature women, whereas Azuma's work was of the more traditional kawaii variety. While not always strictly pornography (apart from his 1992 strip *Kusari*) Azuma's manga contained sexual elements and paved the way for more pornographic manga magazines—such as *Manga Burikko* and *Lemon People* — to feature prepubescent girls. The target audience is — predictably — male, white-collar workers in their 20s and 30s.

The main thrust of lolicon stories include taboo relationships, such as between a teacher and student, brother and sister; or sexual experimentation between two children. Female mangaka Kaworu Watashiya's *Kodomo No Jikan* (*Nymphet*) is an example of a series that, while not pornographic, is still an extremely sensitive subject —that of a nine-year-old girl who develops a crush on her teacher. The series was originally licensed for distribution in North America in 2006 by Seven Seas Entertainment, but was ultimately pulled as it was deemed too controversial for an American audience, despite no sex scenes occurring in the series.

Author and sociologist Sharon Kinsella has suggested that lolicon evolved out of the popularity of 1980s manga created by female artists for women, such as the cross-dressing heroine, Lady Oscar, from Riyoko Ikeda's *The Rose of Versailles*. She believed that men followed these styles and started developing their own fan-fiction. As the genre developed, it moved from these cute, tough heroines toward depictions of girls as sexual victims: naked, helpless, fearful, and sometimes bound or chained. This was expanded into computer games and animated videos.

Japanese anime director and Oscar-winner Hayao Miyazaki said in a 1988 *Animage* interview that he preferred to make his protagonists girls, but "it's difficult. They immediately become the subjects of lolicon gokko [a play toy for Lolita complex fans]. In a sense, if we want to depict someone who is a positive role model, we have no choice but to make them as lovely as possible. But now, there are too many people who shamelessly depict [the heroines] as if they just want [the girls] as pets, and things are escalating more and more."

Left:
A stylized depiction by Junko Mizuno.

Opposite page, left:
"Of course, I was influenced by all the Japanese 'cute' stuff," revealed Junko Mizuno. "It's almost impossible to avoid them if you grow up in Japan. But I also like many other different things such as horror movies, fetish art, Buddhist art, etc. I'm even influenced by TV shows, fashion magazines, toys, food, conversations with people…almost everything that surrounds me."

Opposite page, top center:
Toshiki Yui's cover to *Hot Tails* #8.

Opposite page, top right:
The fairly inoffensive cover to *The New Bondage Fairies* #8 by Kondom.

Opposite page, bottom right:
Kondom's *Bondage Fairies* series featured nymphs having sex with all manner of creatures, from grasshoppers to squirrels. Here, the western translation parodies Stan Lee's writing style for 1960s' Marvel Comics, adding a dimension of humor to the bizarre scene.

SHONEN-AI

Shonen-ai literally means "boy love" and is manga that focuses more on romance, rather than explicit sexual content. Shonen-ai started out as a shojo (girls') sub-genre in the early 1970s, with titles like Keiko Takemiya's *Kaze To Ki No Uta* (Song of the Wind and Trees), which took place in the romantic setting of late 19th century Europe. As one editor noted in Frederik L. Schodt's *Manga! Manga!* book, "Love between boys in another country is so completely distant from [adolescent girls'] own reality that it's not threatening, yet it still gives them a vicarious experience."

One of the most popular shonen-ai mangas of all-time is Akimi Yoshida's *Banana Fish*. A simultaneously brutal and humorous tale of gang warfare in 1980s New York, it featured a slow-burning romance between the two male protagonists, gang leader Ash Lynx and Japanese photographer's assistant Eiji Okamura. Because of the action sequences and excellent storytelling the homoerotic tale had a huge crossover audience, despite very adult themes — such as Ash's past as a "sex toy" of his criminal mentor Papa Golzine. The series was translated by Viz Media into English in a staggering 19 volumes, each one 192 pages long.

Another shonen-ai that was recently translated by DC Comics' CMX manga line in the United States is *From Eroica With Love*, about an openly gay English lord and art thief—the ridiculously named Dorian Red Gloria—also known as Eroica, whose purpose is "to pursue and capture beautiful things...and people."

The actual term shonen-ai is pretty much obsolete in Japan these days, and the more popular phrase "Boy's Love" is being used instead to describe this romantic gay stories. But invariably romance and love leads to sex and—in typical Japanese compartmentalism—this spawned yet another subgenre, *yaoi* manga.

Oppsite page:
Cover to shonen-ai magazine, *June*.
Launched in 1978, the "Boy's Love"
magazine sells around 80,000 copies
a month, to a mostly female readership.

Left:
This 2005 cover from the gay comic,
Bakudan, (published by Furukawa) is
by Gengoroh Tagame. "On magazine
covers, the publishers require very 'soft'
images, but these kind of innocuous
pin-ups are not so interesting to draw,"
revealed the artist.

Above:
Yu-shin~Virtus (*Virtues~Manliness*) first
appeared in *Gekidan* magazine in 2005.
The story is about Roman gladiators,
and it struck a middle ground between
true gay comics and Yaoi titles.
"I really enjoyed drawing this
'romantic' love story,"
explained Tagame.

YAOI

The yaoi genre focuses predominantly on male/ male sexual relationships and is marketed at older women. In Japan, it is better known as "Boys' Love" or "BL." Originally, much of the material was called Junè, named after the 1978 anthology that launched the genre. It featured male/male "tanbi" romances (the old fashioned term for the worship and pursuit of beauty), with stories written using flowery language and gentle graphics, inherited from the shojo manga. Yaoi was originally named after the English letters in the acronym of the Japanese phrase, YAma nashi, Ochi nashi, Imi nashi, "no climax, no point, no meaning." The term appeared as early as the 1970s to describe any self-published doujinshi that was a bizarre, playful parody. However, it has since been associated with sexually explicit homosexual stories.

Although the genre is marketed at women and girls, a portion of gay and bisexual men also read BL titles such as *Be X Boy* and *Dear+* and Japanese mangaka, such as Kodaka Kazuma, are careful to distinguish their works as yaoi, rather than gay, when describing them to Westerners.

Yaoi has become hugely popular in the West on the back of its more mainstream cousins. So much so that there are numerous Western creators drawing new stories, and even several conventions dedicated to the genre across America, such as Yaoi-Con in San Francisco which has seen attendance triple since its launch in 2001. What started as a small subculture has, in the last three years, become a burgeoning market, with new publishers such as Yaoi Press, Better With Boys Press, and Yaoi House emerging. In 2006, Dramaqueen publishers debuted their quarterly anthology *RUSH*, featuring art from global creators. Japanese yaoi is also regularly translated across the world by companies such as Digital Manga Publishing's imprints 801 Media and June, as well as Dramaqueen, Kitty Media, and Tokyo Pop's adult BLU imprint.

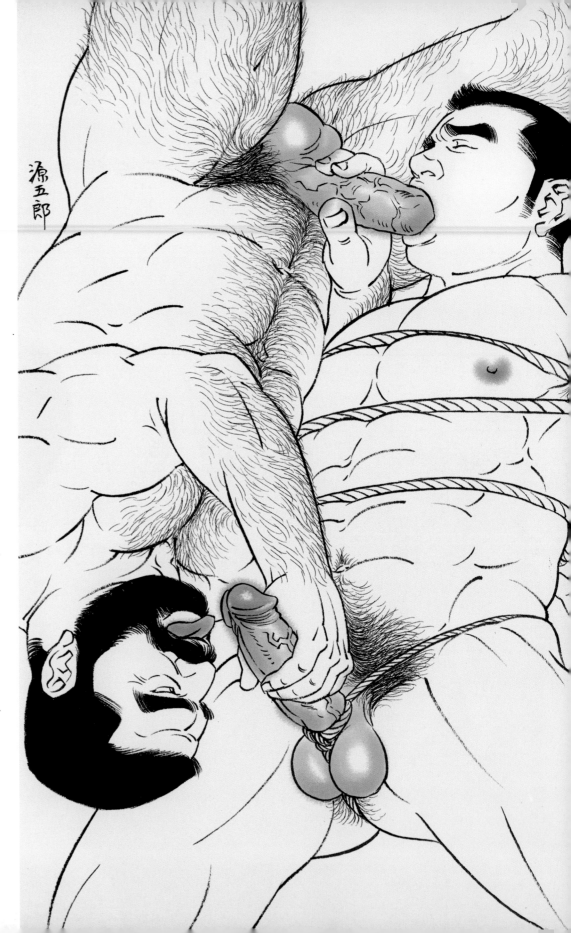

Opposite page:
Originally published in 2000's *Sabu* magazine, Tagame's *Akafun-jigoku* (*The Red Loincloth Inferno*) was partly inspired by old shunga prints and traditional Japanese brush work.

Left:
Kimi-yo-shiru-ya-minami-no-goku? (*Do You Remember the South Island's P.O.W. Camp?*) was originally serialized in *G-men* magazine between 2001-2006. The story explored sexual abuses in a US-led WW2 P.O.W. camp, but strangely mirrored the events at the Abu Gharib prison in Iraq. "This story is one of my most important works," said Tagame, "Because drawing the ugliness of our world is an important theme for me."

Above:
The story, *Sarashi-dai*, by gay Japanese artist Tagame. "The beauty of cruelty is another very important theme in my work. I am drawn to the historical tortures in all countries, and this story is about one example, the pillory." This strip was published in *Nikutaiha* in 2008, though his work doesn't always make print.

TENTACLE PORN

One of the more surreal and outlandish sexual subgenres to permeate Japanese manga and anime is what is crudely referred to as "Tentacle Porn," which is the generally non-consensual penetration of a person (male or female) by either octopuses, squids, or, more usually, evil demons or aliens with multiple tentacles. As one pundit put it, "the Japanese can fetish-ize anything."

But this is not a new phenomenon. As far back as the Edo period, shunga masters like Katsushika Hokusai (1760-1849) were creating scenes like the notorious *The Dream of the Fisherman's Wife*, created in 1814. Hokusai was the artist who first coined the term manga (meaning "whimsical" or "irresponsible drawings"), and his famous image of a woman having sex with an octopus inspired numerous Japanese fine artists to follow suit including Masami Teraoka's 2002 work *Sarah and Octopus/Seventh Heaven* and Toshio Saeki's *Octo-girl*. Saeki — Japan's master of erotic illustration — explained his run-ins with the law.

"My books have received cautions from the local government agency that monitors such things," revealed Saeki, in a 2001 interview with Stephen Lemons. "If you receive three cautions in a year, your book is prohibited from being sold in a bookstore. Of course, my publications have been unpopular with the police, but not enough to be banned," said the godfather of Japanese erotica.

This seemingly niche fetish became more mainstream in Japan with the release of Toshio Maeda's 1986 *Urotsukidōji* saga (Better known as *Legend of the Overfiend* in the West). It is a story of demons and "man-beasts" merging with the human world, so that all women become never-dressed prostitutes, ever happy to perform sexual acts on any man. The main reason for tentacle erotica is Article 175's ban on depicting penises and so inventive anime and manga artists have used the tentacle as a replacement. "At that time it was illegal to create a sensual scene in bed. I thought I should do something to avoid drawing such a normal sensual scene. So I just created a creature.

[His tentacle] is not a [penis]. I could say, as an excuse, this is not a [penis], this is just a part of the creature. You know, the creatures, they don't have a gender. A creature is a creature. So it is not obscene — not illegal," Maeda spuriously justified.

Before *Urotsukidōji* , Maeda was already infamous for his frank depictions of sex and violence in his work. He had grown tired of the cliché-ridden world of early erotic manga, and was looking to take the genre into a new direction. "I really wanted to create something different, but the editor wanted me to create some regular manga for adults — like a typical type of salaryman falling in love with an office lady...a boring story. But I just wanted to make something different. The chief editor was against my idea, but I insisted," the artist recounted.

Maeda's manga was adapted into an controversial anime film and the artist/writer went on to create even more perverse tentacle-related works such as *Demon Beast Invasion*, *Injukyoshi* (aka Obscene Beast Teacher) and *La Blue Girl*, with the latter even becoming a live action version.

But tentacle rape hasn't remained on Far Eastern shores. In September, 2007 Marvel Comics in the United States caused a furor when it published a cover to *Heroes for Hire* #13, painted by respected female Japanese manga artist Sana Takeda. It featured the three heroines tied up in extremely submissive poses, with their clothes loosened and sweat and slime dripping down them. Several tentacles were seen making their way toward the unfortunate trio. Fans slammed Marvel for portraying "hentai tentacle porn" on the cover of a comic intended for 13+ year-olds, and the misogynist nature of the image — an argument the publisher failed to successfully counter. It's probably this aspect of tentacle porn that gives it such a bad reputation, as so much of it is based on rape fantasies and non-consensual sex, and definitely reveals a darker side to manga's psyche.

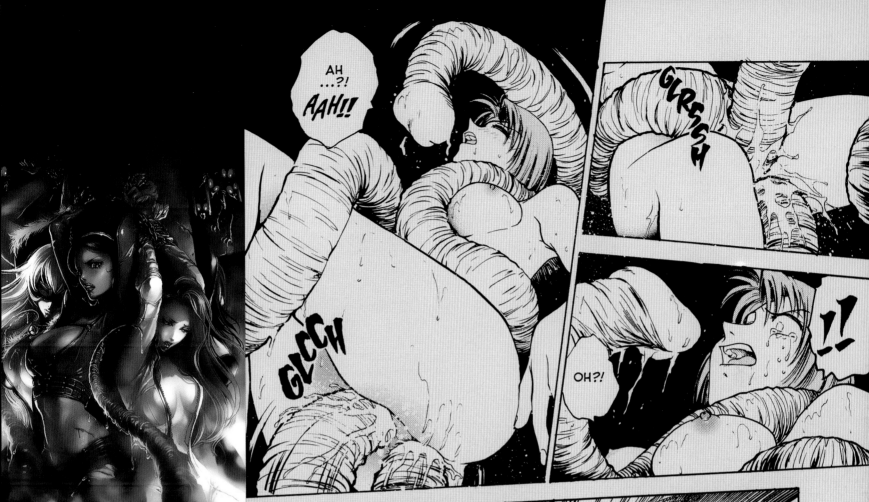

Opposite page:
The Dream of The Fisherman's Wife shunga print, by Hokusai, is one of the earliest surviving examples of "tentacle sex."

Above:
This cover to *Heroes for Hire* #13 by female mangaka Sana Takeda caused controversy in the USA when published.

Right:
A dream sequence from *S & M University*, by Nariaki Funabori, has one of the main characters, Yuki, attacked by five tentacle/penis creatures.

FUTANARI AND BAKUNYU

Other niche manga fetishes include *futanari* and *bakunyu*. Futanari ("two form") manga specializes in erotic tales of hermaphrodites, intersex, or characters with both sets of genitalia. Also referred to as "dickgirls" or "shemales," futanari are more politely known as "newhalf." It is generally drawn in a cutesy anime style, such as Q's *Behind Moon*, Haruki Genia's *Raijinkai*, and the less explicit *Boku No Futatsu No Tsubasa* (*My Two Wings*) by Toshiki Yui.

A specific fetish within the futanari subgenre is having characters having objects inserted into their urethra from which the futanari derives sexual pleasure. But when two futa characters get together one futa impossibly inserts her penis into the other's urethra.

Futanari obviously shares the same fetish as Western shemale pornography, but its execution shares more with the yuri (lesbian) genre and is an extension of the lesbian theme where a strap-on dildo is used. This allows storylines to take a more lesbian context, which is more appealing to straight Japanese males.

There are numerous hentai manga and anime that feature futanari, including the wonderfully descriptive *Alice In Sexland*, *Bondage Game*, *Dickgirl Bride*, *Erotic Torture Chamber*, *Hot Tails*, *Pink Sniper Maniax*, *Project Boobs*, *Shemale Behavior*, and *Sister, Sperm, Glasses*.

As in most types of hentai, there is some overlap between fetishes, and futanari is no exception, often combining with bukkake, BDSM, catgirl, lolicon, and tentacle sex. Often futanari characters have almost comedically enormous phalluses which have a similar appeal to those of another fetish, "bakunyu"— women or futanari with huge breasts — and the two fetishes frequently cross over.

Bakunyu focuses on women with unfeasibly large breasts (literally "bursting breasts") and most likely relates to the Japanese desire for all things Western, as the majority of Japanese woman have smaller breasts than their Caucasian cousins. This is in the same vein as Japanese retailers selling pre-padded panties to give women a fuller, "Western" bottom. Bakunyu stories are not just about sex — although that is a central theme — and many focus on the male protagonist's relationship with his object d'amour as it builds over a long time. This "romantic" approach usually results in them having sex.

Bakunyu are also not limited to only heterosexual relationships — they may also contain some lesbian (yuri) manga as well. Examples are *Blue Eyes*, a nine-volume hentai manga created by Tohru Nishimaki, and *Anyone You Can Do...I Can Do Better*, a two-part bakunyu anime (part of the *Milk Junkies* series aka Boobalicious in the United States) which features a male tutor who is hired to teach a very well endowed girl whom he predictably seduces, along with her equally mammoth-mammaried mother.

Opposite page, bottom left
The character's oversized breasts are the primary focus on this page from *God of Sex*, by Kazuki Taniuchi.

Opposite page, top right:
A futanari (shemale) in *Silky Whip* #10 by the pseudonymous mangaka known as "Oh! Great" aka Ito Ogure.

Opposite page, bottom right:
Yukiyanagi's *Milk Mama* collected numerous mammary adventures, including this tale of a boy who has been breast-fed all his life and ultimately engages in an incestuous relationship with his mother. This page reads in Eastern order, from top to bottom, right to left.

Right:
This cover painting to *Silky Whip* #5 by Oh! Great obviously plays to the bakunyu audience with the wet T-shirt.

THE DARK SIDE OF DESIRE

In 1989, things went terribly wrong for erotic manga. There came a major crackdown after the infamous — and horrific — kidnapping, murder, and sexual molestation of three pre-school girls by Tsutomu Miyazaki, an Otaku (an obsessive fan-boy), who was a huge devotee of lolicon manga. The Tokyo High Court ruled him sane, stating that "the murders were premeditated and stemmed from Miyazaki's sexual fantasies," and he was sentenced to death.

This case caused a furor in parents' and teachers' groups concerned over the sexual and violent content of certain manga. A Japanese non-profit organization called CASPAR claimed that lolicon and other anime did encourage sex crimes. The group campaigns for regulation of minors in pornographic magazines and video games. According to Michiko Magaoko, director of a non-profit organization in Kyoto called

Juvenile Guide, founded in 2003, approximately half of the staggering 2,000 pornographic anime titles distributed in Japan every year, include schoolgirl characters. The Osaka-based Child Protection Agency's Mitsui Kondo argues that the films distort attitudes toward girls: "Such a situation makes our society more dangerous to girls...We've got to think about it before talking about freedom of expression."

However, the Miyazaki murders are still exceptional, and the island state has far fewer incidents of rape and murder than America. To counter the general public's outrage over the schoolgirls' murders, the manga industry set-up the self-regulatory group the Association to Protect Freedom of Expression in Comics. Headed by several high-profile mangaka (comic professionals), they went on a counter-offensive, fighting for creative freedom and attacking censorship. It eventually worked, and by 1994 the manga witch hunt was off, as Japan's moral minority trooped off to right wrongs elsewhere. As one pundit put it, "There was a big fuss about it for a while, but now everything seems pretty much the way it's always been."

The eminent sexologists Milton Diamond and Ayako Uchiyama observed a strong link between the dramatic rise of pornographic material in Japan from the 1970s onwards and a dramatic decrease in reported sexual violence, including crimes by juveniles and assaults on children under 13. They also cited similar findings in Denmark and West Germany, believing that countries' concerns with widespread availability of sexually explicit material leading to increased rates of sexual crimes was not valid. They went so far as to say that the reduction of sexual crimes in Japan during that period may have been influenced by a variety of factors, including erotic manga. As Alan Moore put it in his article on pornography in *Arthur* magazine, the porn acted as "a safety valve on a pressure cooker."

Left:
Kazuki Taniuchi's *God of Sex* reveals how explicit manga has become. In Japan, lip service would have been paid by a small black bar placed over the penetration shot in the first panel — this is removed for western audiences.

Above:
This erotic fantasy is one of the less predatory stories from Toshiki Yui's *Hot Tails* series.

Opposite page, left:
The cover to *Co-Ed Sexxtasy* #13 by Makoto Fujisaki illustrates the huge popularity of bondage and submissive comics in Japan. The apples and oranges suggest "forbidden fruit."

Opposite page, top right:
A *Co-Ed Sexxtasy* scene about two students, Akira and Nagi, and their diverse sex life.

Opposite page, bottom right:
Notice in this orgy from *Silky Whip* that the men are drawn semi-realistically — and slightly sinister looking — while the woman maintains the kwaii ("cute") aesthetic.

Alongside numerous other reasons — including a high sense of social responsibility in Japanese society — many have argued that because the Japanese so openly explore their deepest, darkest fantasies in manga, animation, and live-action film, very few individuals ever feel the need to act them out. Titles like the pernicious *Rapeman* act as a cathartic release for readers, and simply put, most Japanese can tell the difference between fantasy and reality. The other anomaly with these sexually violent comics is that the vast portion are created by women and, if examined closely, actually put the woman in a position of power rather than being the victim, further confusing the issue.

In 2004, the whole censorship issue kicked off again when, on January 13, Suwa Yuuji's (under the pseudonym "Beauty Hair") pornographic *Misshitsu* (*The Honey Room*) was deemed "obscene" by Judge Yujiro Nagatani of the Tokyo district court. *The Honey Room* was originally published in 2002 with an initial print of 20,000 copies, sold across Japan.

The court's objection, under Article 175 of the Penal Code, was to "bodies [that] were drawn in a lifelike manner with little attention to concealment [of genitalia], making for sexually explicit expression and deeming the book pornographic matter," said the judge. Nagatani also stated the manga was "mostly devoted to undisguised, detailed portrayals of sex scenes" that "no healthy society today could allow." The publishers defended *The Honey Room* on the grounds of freedom of expression and argued that drawings could not be considered as lifelike as photographs or video images. But the judge handed Motonori Kishi — the president of publishing house Shobunkan — a one-year prison term. To avoid a custodial sentence, Kishi reluctantly accepted the guilty verdict, and the sentence was reduced to a ¥1.5-million-yen ($14,000 US) fine in June 2005.

The first major obscenity trial in Japan for 20 years sent shockwaves around the manga world, with many artists and publishers self-censoring, as before, and shops scrapping their adult-only manga sections. The case rumbled along for some time, but in his final appeal in 2007, the Supreme Court's First Petty Bench denied Motonori Kishi's appeal, meaning the publisher had to pay his ¥1.5-million fine. Even then, once the press lost interest, everything carried on much as it has since the 1700s. Rightly or wrongly, extreme erotic manga continues to proliferate in Japan, and abroad, as its more innocent forbearers' popularity continues to grow.

Opposite page, top left:
A previously unpublished convention poster created by Hiroyuki Utatane, the artist on highly regarded erotic series *Countdown: Sex Bombs* and the more mainstream *Seraphic Feather.* The lithe bodies have caused some to suggest many manga characters are pre-pubescent, but this fails to take the artists' drawing styles into consideration.

Opposite page, top right:
A scene from *Sex-Philes*—a series of short sexual vignettes—by Benkya Tamaoki, has a lactating slave, Alice. The series was published in the US by Eros Comix's Mangerotica sub-imprint.

Left:
The cover to possibly Japan's most controversial manga to date, *Missitsu* (*Honey Room*) by Beauty Hair (aka Suwa Yuuji).

5

Online comics eroticism

WEBCOMICS: OFF PRINT AND ONLINE

Just as Johannnes Gutenberg's invention of the printing press in 1440 and the invention of the photocopier in the 1970s revolutionized the dissemination of ideas, art, and literature, so the invention of the Internet in the 1990s made comic publishing completely egalitarian and global. In all three cases some of the earliest users of these new technologies were artists and pornographers.

But some of the earliest online comics to be published were non-erotic: *Where the Buffalo Roam* by Hans Bjordahl in 1992; *Doctor Fun* by David Farley in 1993; and *Argon Zark!* by Charley Parker, launched in 1995. The latter was the first ongoing story specifically designed for the Internet, as opposed to an existing strip scanned in. Whereas many lesser-known creators perhaps self-published only a few hundred comics, the new technology suddenly gave them access to millions of potential readers.

But what online cartoonists really found liberating was the complete freedom to explore

any subject, completely unfettered. It was akin to the underground comix movement of the '60s where artists pushed the medium as far as they could, with some webcomics stretching the boundaries of taste, taking advantage of the fact that Internet censorship is virtually nonexistent.

The freedom of webcomics can still cause problems though, as *Leisure Town* artist Tristan Farnon found when he had legal trouble after creating a homoerotic parody of newspaper cartoon *Dilbert*. In 1997, Farnon scanned *Dilbert* strips and changed the speech balloons to deliberately inflammatory racist and profane dialog. Farnon played cat-and-mouse with United Media's lawyers (the copyright holders), constantly taking down and reposting the strips over the next eight years. "You realize that when you make online comics, you're sort of folding up your product into a paper airplane and sailing it out the window, and who knows who's going to catch it," mused Farnon, later.

Partly inspired by Scott McCloud's book *Reinventing Comics*, 2000 saw an explosion of webcomics. Soon "anthology" portals offer a variety of professional and small press creators' strips, with sites like *Cool Beans World Modern Tales* and *Web Comics Nation* popping up everywhere. By 2007 a staggering 15,000 webcomics were being posted on a regular basis — some good, some diabolical. This, combined with numerous pirate websites that offer illegal scans of printed erotic comics, has made it hard for many erotic comic publishers, who have seen sales decline. As Eric Reynolds of Fantagraphics/Eros Comix — one of the US's biggest publishers of erotic sequential art — noted, "erotic comics sales in general have slowed considerably in this era of Internet porn, and we've cut back to all but the most profitable titles..."

SAFFYRE BLUE

ISSUE 0
APR '08

WWW.
HIP
COMIX
.COM

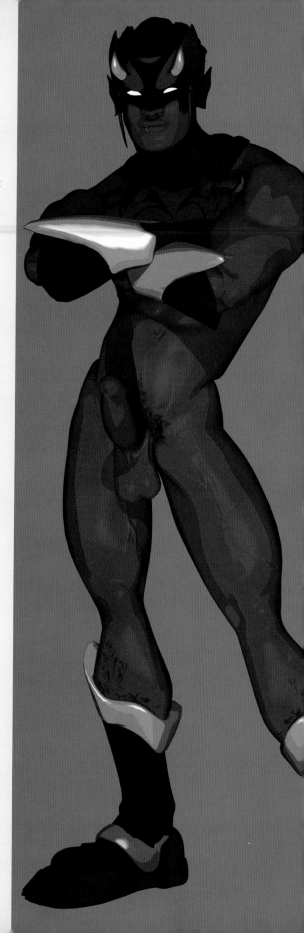

Previous page:
Online cartoonist and designer, Jess Fink's powerfully lustful cover to *Eros Comix Head* #14.

Opposite page, left:
Morpheus' cover to his online erotic fantasy, *Saffyre Blue*, from the website *HipComix.com*.

Opposite page, right:
A digitally rendered character study by Joe Phillips of his gay superhero Stonewall — referring to the infamous Greenwich Village tavern where the gay rights movement started. The hero appears in comic creator Phillips' computer animated movie, *Stonewall and Riot: The Ultimate Orgasm*. The artist was one of the first to fully exploit the Internet's possibilities by posting online comics and computer animated shorts on his website, joephillips.com.

Above:
Two pages from Morpheus' short story, *Obsession*, from *HipComix.com*. The dark voyeuristic/exhibitionist strip was hand drawn, but computer colored "I still prefer to pencil and ink in the traditional way." explained the artist, "then scan in and color in Photoshop or Painter."

Left:
A scene from *Stonewall and Riot* in which Stonewall gives supervillian Polecat his "stiff shaft of justice." Phillips managed to retain his art style while using computer animation.

GAY COMICS ONLINE

Every sexual proclivity is available as a webcomic, and obviously there is a large proportion of high-quality gay comics on the Internet. One of the better titles was the popular manga-inspired series, *Boy Meets Boy*, by K. Sandra Fuhr, which ran for four years from September 2000. Nominated several times for the Web Cartoonist's Choice Award, it finally won in 2003.

Another classic gay-themed strip was versatile cartoonist/editor Tim Fish's *Young Bottoms in Love* on the PopImage website. Created in August 2002 as an online daily comic, *Young Bottoms In Love* examined gay romance from nearly every angle, with dozens of creators — gay and straight, amateur and professional — contributing stories, both funny and poignant. The impressive roster of artists included Paige Braddock, Adam DeKraker, David Kelley, and curbsider Robert Kirby.

When the strip was finally wrapped up four years later "...both Tim and I thought it would be amazing if we could convince Howard Cruse to contribute the final strip," said PopImage co-editor-in-chief, Ed Mathews. The result was Cruse's six-page strip, *My Hypnotist*, which ensured the strip finished with a bang, rather than a whimper.

Fish has since completed several printed projects, most notably his 550-page *Cavalcade*

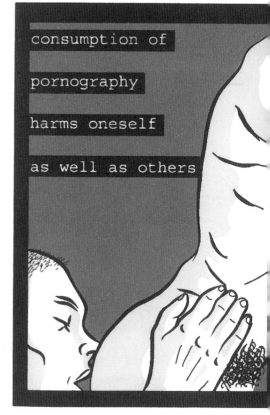

of Boys graphic novel in 2006. Fish's art style has developed to become an intriguing mixture of Image co-founder Erik Larsen and saucy '50s gag cartoonist and *Archie* artist, Dan DeCarlo, and *Cavalcade* is serilized in Boston's LGBT newspaper, Bay Windows.

Another major gay writer is Chicago-based Dale Lazarov, who has produced numerous gay erotica including *STICKY*, drawn by Steve MacIsaac, which was published by Eros in 2005 and collected by Bruno Gmünder Verlag in 2006. Despite his standing as a quality writer of intelligent gay erotica, Lazarov confessed, "I secretly want to both write the ultimate art comix graphic novel, as well as a fondly remembered run on [DC Comics'] *Legion of Super-Heroes*."

His homoerotic fantasy strip collaboration with Delic Van Loond, *Fancy*, was serialized as a webcomic at AdultWebcomics.com, the online home of many great cartonists, including Jess Fink.

Top center:
Two scenes from Joe Philips' online homoerotic animation, *The House of Morecock*. The short, humorous films—about a paranormal investigator, Jonas Morecock—were collected into a graphic novel with new stories added.

Right:
Steve MacIsaac, deliberately juxtaposed classic counter-pornography text with implicit imagery, making a sexually political statement in his self-published *Mantras* strip from *Shirtlifter* #0. MacIsaac is a gay online cartoonist who regularly posts stories on *adultwebcomics.com*.

Opposite page, right:
Gay comix legend Howard Cruse wrote and drew *My Hypnotist*—the last strip to appear on the high quality, but sadly defunct, webcomic, *Young Bottoms in Love*.

pornography
encourages
abuse and
degradation
and violence

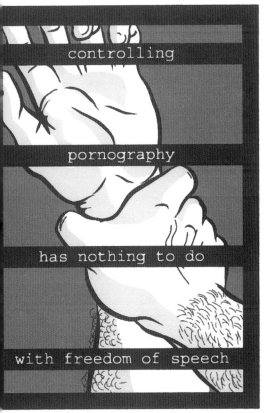

controlling

pornography

has nothing to do

with freedom of speech

SEXYLOSERS.COM

There are thousands of erotic comic websites, with the majority focusing on sensational art, depicting graphic scenes akin to Spanish and Japanese erotic comics. Typically, the most prevalent are hentai; and Japanese manga and anime have more sites than anyone else.

Sexy Losers was a strip that was heavily inspired by manga styles and themes — as are many of the younger, new wave of comic creators. Launched in April 1999, and written and drawn by Clay, the title dealt with all manner of sexual peccadilloes. It took extreme sex situations and turned them on their head, deliberately handling them in a flip, off-hand manner. A good example of this is the ongoing theme of necrophilia, which both a father and son enjoy. *Sexy Losers* has had a longer run than most webcomics and has achieved enough of an audience to run on and off for nine years.

Poonnet.com is a site run by various erotic artists; and styles and subject matters

vary from she-males to celebrity parodies, but it predominantly focuses on interracial sex. Another site, *Dirtycomics.com*, is a better than average site with the sexy, yet silly, *Fiona's Time Machine* standing out, as the story of a woman trapped in history with a time-traveling dildo.

New technologies have led to new art techniques, and the advent of software such as Poser and Maya has allowed artists to create three-dimensional figures, with realistic lighting and skin tones. While the art is of a distinctly varying quality, there is a tendency for technology to replace talent and storytelling. One of the biggest problems is that 3D figures tend to look cold and sterile, like much of the photographic pornography created today. Consequently, most of the strips lack the humor and warmth of their hand-drawn counterparts and are usually barren emotionless tableaux, which are about as erotic as two naked mannequins lying on top of each other.

Below:
Saffyre Blue fights off a naked creature. Morpheus explained his reasons for using CGI graphics in his strips; "At the beginning it was mainly a time consideration. When creating hand-drawn art I have to pencil, ink, color, and letter and there's ample scope at each stage to screw up the finished art and send you back to the start. With CGI you have the magic of the "undo" command… In many ways I consider the art of creating CGI strips to be akin to being a film director—the artist creates the set, adds the cast, sets up lighting, moves the camera to get the best angle… just as the director does."

Opposite page:
Online artist Morpheus' feisty heroine, Saffyre Blue, finds herself at the mercy of a villain. "She is the result of my love for female warrior fantasy strips like *Barbarella*, *Axa*, and *Druuna*, but with a *Heavy Metal*-style twist and she popped into my head more or less fully formed about 15 years ago." However it wasn't until he went online that he found the perfect medium.

JESS FINK

Jess Fink had always made erotic drawings in lush, long, curvaceous lines, so when one of her college professors told her about Eros Comix the New York School of Visual Arts graduate thought, "Hey, I want to make money doing comics!" She got in touch, and started working for the Seattle-based publisher in 2004. "As it turns out, you don't really make all that much money doing it."

Fink successfully collaborated with writer Polly Frost on several strips and comics for Eros, and her beautiful full-color artwork has been featured in several anthologies, including *Blowjob*, *Rear Entry*, and culminating in the entire issue of *Head* #14 in 2006.

Fink is refreshingly open and honest about her erotic comics output, and is distinctly unabashed. "Artists have this weird bias toward porno," she says. "Sex is just as good a topic for art as anything." Just like her parents' generation of underground cartoonists, Fink was also inspired by the lewd *Tijuana Bible* mini-comics of the 1920s. "They're just really, really dirty...Popeye has this humongous penis, and he has sex with Olive Oyl and it comes out her mouth. It's great."

But it's online where Fink shines the most, with her *Dirty Limericks* webcomic, appearing regularly on *Adultwebcomics.com*. These smutty and silly vignettes told in rhyming couplets recount a variety of sexcapades, including a woman pretending to be a man to sleep with gay boys and the occasional straight girl.

2007 saw the launch of a new erotic webcomic, *Chester 5000 XYV*, about a love robot whose job is to satisfy a decadent and demanding lady. Originally a gift from her absent husband, it turns wrong when passionate jealousies rise to the fore. But generally Fink's erotic comics are enjoyable affairs, "I like it when people have new ideas about what sexy is," says Fink. "I like presenting that in a happy way."

Fink relishes filling the void of good porn for women. "Whenever I think of other women doing porn I always think it's going to

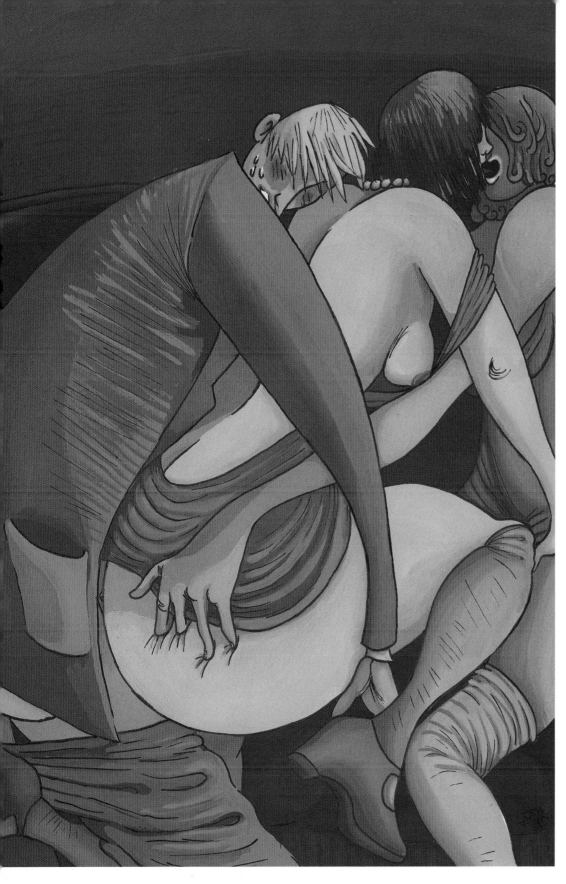

Opposite page and above:
Pages from Jess Fink's strip *The Grand Finale*,
part of her *Dirty Limericks* series that appeared
on *Adultwebcomics.com*. This was the first strip
the artist had published by Eros Comix.

Left:
Jess Fink's arousing, yet implicit, cover to
Rear Entry #9 (2005).

be really flowery and bad. Like romance novels
or something...girly, nondescriptive," she
explained. "I like really graphic stuff. If it's porn,
I want it to be porn...I don't want to talk down
to women, like, 'I know you don't like sex so I'll
make this easy on you. Women are attracted to
characters, things that feel real," said Fink, who
gets lots of comments from women thanking
her for making her male characters more
attractive — her work is full of metrosexuals
and pretty-boy artists —"I like effeminate
men," she explains, "Maybe [short, fat, and
hairy porn star] Ron Jeremy is someone's idea
of attractive, but..."

Above and opposite page:
Chester 5000 XYV, by Jess Fink, first appeared online at *Adultwebcomics.com* as a five-page story as part of her *Dirty Limericks* series, but developed into a ongoing narrative in February 2007.

Jess Fink's work on *Adultcomics.com* is some of the best on the erotic comics website, which acts as a hub for many other talented creators. Other strips of note include the "pop art porn" of Laura O'Callaghan-White's strip, *Bukkake*, which is pure unadulterated filthy fun, drawn in a bright Roy Lichtenstien style.

Isaac Priestley, who had already drawn the series *Progressions*, started his *Chastity Towers* series in 2007. It's a classic tale of sexual experimentation in a girls' finishing school, in the vein of Francisco Solano López's *Young Witches*.

The anal antics of Lucy Luvbottom are reminiscent of the late Art Wetherall's work for Eros, and feature the volutiously proportioned damsel of the derriere constantly looking for anal sex, in any shape or form. Its over-the-top sense of humor dissipates the shock value of the well-crafted artwork. As artist Dezi X explained, "Always the optimist, she sees an opportunity for anal adventure in every situation!"

Meanwhile, J.L. Roberson's series, *This Sickness*, recounts the funny, but intensily graphic bisexual Mistress, Rosa, and her slave, Annaliese. Roberson's other strip, *Vladruska*, about a fictional Soviet porn star, is a sharp satire on the old Russia and cleverly uses techniques remiscent of an old Eisenstein film.

Possibly the best strip on the website, both in terms of the quality of art and hilarity factor, was Chris Jones' *Grumps* (*www.grumps.ca*) — obviously inspired by Ren & Stimpy creator John Kricfalusi's cartoons. The "old school depravity" featured two pensioners, Horris and Mr. Smits, in a nursing home as they constantly perv at the buxom nurses and try and sink their pink torpedoes into the fellow female residents one last time before they die. Sadly the series ended in June, 2008. Jones' other webcomics include *Byron Pinkleton*, a hysterical, historical piece of tosh and the sex-mad superhero *Captain Excelsior* (*www.captainexcelsior.com*), who can't keep it in his pants for longer than five minutes.

THE EROTIC ADVENTURES OF SPACE BABE 113

John Maybury's *The Erotic Adventures of Space Babe 113* is a "naughty SF comedy" that owes a debt to previous sexy space sirens of the past, such as Jean-Claude Forest's 1960s strip *Barbarella*, with the light, humorous tones of Harvey Kurtzman and Will Elder's *Little Annie Fannie*. Artistically speaking, Maybury's influences come from further afield, with Japanese mangaka Junko Mizuno being an acknowledged inspiration. "I love her stuff, it's dark, sexy, cute, and stylish," he explained. There's a touch of erotic underground cartoonist Vaughn Bodé, as well. The minimalist art manages to convey a sexy, voluptuous woman, without the explicitness.

Space Babe is the catering officer on the trading spaceship Marco Polo, who — inadvertently, and invariably — gets entangled in various sexy misadventures with the ship's misfit crew. On her departure she promised her boyfriend she would be celibate for the five-year-long mission, but it proves a challenge.

Space Babe's humor derives from old British *Carry On…* movies, and typically saucy, tongue-in-cheek absurdity. For example, she wears "standard-issue European Space Force knickers, equipped with on-board artificial intelligence, which can perform the functions of a PDA and can connect to various wireless networks." They also talk back to her.

Originally published by Soaring Penguin in the UK, as an ongoing series in a "US comics with the top chopped off" format, these black and white tales have adapted, and with stories created for the revolutionary, non-erotic, *Rokcomics.com*, which allows users to download comics onto their mobile phones.

Interestingly, Maybury also employs the latest technology to create his comic, first drawing it on a touchscreen PDA, then uploading the artwork to his PC where he converts the bitmap images to vector drawings. He then letters and colors the strip, assembling each panel.

So, the Internet has meant that fans of erotica need never leave the house and face the potential embarrassment of buying material in the shops, either by purchasing them from online stores, or by downloading them directly. Anime, hentai, erotic comics, and the like are now available to all. Whether this is a good thing is a moot point, as it continually perpetuates the shame factor of pornography, rather than the acceptance that there can be such a thing as — as Alan Moore puts it — "good porn," that is healthy, happy, non-exploitative, shameless erotica for all genders and sexual persuasions. Something that maybe, one day, society will work towards.

Opposite page:
A complete adventure — *Review* — of *Space Babe 113* by John Maybury. The repetitive square panels are a result of the creator working on a PDA and formatting the strip so that it can be read on a mobile phone, after being downloaded from *Rokcomics.com*.

ART DIRECTORY

This book is an historical retrospective, critique, and review of erotic comic art. Every effort has been made to trace and acknowledge all copyright and trademark holders, and obtain permissions for the works reproduced in this book. The author and publishers sincerely apologize for any inadvertent errors or omissions and will be happy to correct them in future editions, but hereby must disclaim any liability.

BIBLIOGRAPHY

While this book manages to pack a lot in, it really is the tip of the iceberg and I would wholeheartedly recommend you seek out the following books for a more in-depth look at the various artists, publishers and creators included herein:

BOOKS

Best Erotic Comics 2008
Greta Christina
Last Gasp, 2008

Manga: Sixty Years of Japanese Comics
Paul Gravett
Laurence King, 2004

Graphic Novels: Stories to Change Your Life
Paul Gravett
Aurum Press, 2005

Sex in the Comics
Maurice Horn
Random House Value Publishing, 1988

Nasty Tales: Sex, Drugs, Rock'n'Roll and Violence in the British Underground
David Huxley
Headpress, 2001

Erotic Comics: A Graphic History Volume 1
Tim Pilcher
Abrams, 2008 (US) / Ilex Press, 2008 (UK)

The Essential Guide to World Comics
Tim Pilcher and Brad Brooks
Collins & Brown, 2005

Comics, Comix & Graphic Novels: A History of Comic Art
Roger Sabin
Phaidon, 2006 edition

Adult Comics
Roger Sabin
Routledge, 1993

Dreamland Japan: Writings on Modern Manga
Frederik L. Schodt
Stone Bridge Press, 2002 edition

Manga! Manga! The World of Japanese Comics
Frederik L. Schodt
Kodansha International Ltd.
1986 edition

Comix: The Underground Revolution
Dez Skinn
Collins & Brown/Quality Communications, 2004

Clean Cartoonists' Dirty Drawings
Craig Yoe
Last Gasp, 2007

PUBLISHERS WEBSITES

Auad Publishing
www.auadpublishing.com

The Comics Journal
www.tcj.com

Denis Kitchen Publishing
www.deniskitchen.com

Eros Comix
www.eroscomix.com

Erotic Review Books
www.eroticprints.org

Fantagraphics Books
www.fantagraphics.com

Heavy Metal
www.heavy-metal.net

Kiss Comix
www.lacupula.com

Knockabout
www.knockabout.com

Leyland Publications
www.leylandpublications.com

Marvel
www.marvel.com

National Lampoon
www.nationallampoon.com

NBM Publishing Inc.
www.nbmpub.com

SQP
www.sqpinc.com

Tabou Editions
www.tabou-editions.com

Top Shelf
www.topshelfcomix.com

Verotik
www.danzig-verotik.com/verotik

ARTIST WEBSITES

Jason Atomic
www.jasonatomic.co.uk

Donna Barr
www.donnabarr.com

Alison Bechdel
www.dykestowatchoutfor.com

Nick Bertozzi
nickbertozzi.com

Barry Blair and Colin Warbridge
www.blairdotcomix.co.uk

Frank Cho
www.libertymeadows.com

Hunt Emerson
www.largecow.com

Patrick Fillion
www.patrickfillion.com

Jess Fink
www.jessfink.com

Phil Foglio
www.girlgeniusonline.com/comic.php

Vittorio Giardino
www.vittoriogiardino.com

Roberta Gregory
www.robertagregory.com

John Higgins
www.turmoilcolour.com

Ralf König
www.ralf-koenig.de

Rich Larson and Steve Fastner
www.fastnerandlarson.com

Scott Lewis
www.lewisart.com

Milo Manara
www.milomanara.com

John Maybury
www.spacebabe113.com

Jimmy Palmiotti
Amanda Conner
www.paperfilms.com
www.amandaconner.com

Joe Phillips
www.joephillips.com

Spain Rodriguez
www.spainrodriguez.com

Lynn Paula Russell
www.lynnpaularussell.com

Paolo E. Serpieri
www.druuna.net

Stan Shaw
www.drawstanley.com

Robert Triptow
www.roberttriptow.com

Reed Waller
www.omahathecatdancer.com

Larry Welz
www.cherrycomics.com

GENERAL WEBSITES

30th Century Comics
www.thirtiethcentury.free-online.co.uk

Adult Comics Database
www.adultcomicsdatabase.com

Adult Web Comics
www.adultwebcomics.com

Comic Book Legal Defense Fund
www.cbldf.org

ComicsResearch.org
www.comicsresearch.org

Gosh Comics
www.goshlondon.blogspot.com

Hip Comix
www.hipcomix.com

Lambiek
www.lambiek.net

Michigan State University's Comic Art Library
www.lib.msu.edu/comics

New York Public Library's Comic Books Research Guide
www.nypl.org/research/chss/grd/resguides/comic

Ohio State University's Cartoon Research Library
www.cartoons.osu.edu/index.php

Sex, Drugs and Comic Books
www.sexdrugsandcomicbooks.blogspot.com

Sex in Art
www.sexinart.net/category/comics

Sexy Losers
www.sexylosers.com

Tom of Finland Foundation
www.tomoffinlandfoundation.org

INDEX

ACKNOWLEDGMENTS

There are so many amazing people to thank for this book it's difficult to know where to start, so I'll start at the beginning. A big hurrah to Giovanna Casotto for her gloriously sexy cover and interior art, and a massive thank you to Enrico Salvini for arranging it all. And a big thanks to Torren Smith and Kim Thompson for arranging the US cover graphics.

My undying gratitude to Alan Moore for his insightful foreword — you really were the cherry on top, and I'm honoured to have you steering at the helm, as you were a major influence on this book.

As ever, this book wouldn't have been possible without the assistance of Gene Kannenberg, Jr., who stoically took my demands for more depraved filth on the chin (as it were). Gene's picture research, scanning, fact-checking and knowledge elevated the book to something we can both be simultaneously ashamed and proud of! Thanks, buddy.

There were so many people to thank on this mammoth task, so, in no particular order: Lynn Paula Russell, Carol Pinkus at Marvel, Rich Larson and Steve Fastner, Melinda Gebbie, Eric Reynolds at Fantagraphics, Kim Thompson and Paul Baresh for all the Eros Comix images and permissions. Toren Smith for the Japanese advice, Howard Jurofsky at *Heavy Metal*, William Vu at *National Lampoon*, Terry Natier at NBM, Steve Robson at Fanfare, Sal Quartuccio at SQP, Denis Kitchen, Charles Brownstein at the Comic Book Legal Defence Fund and Chris Staros at Top Shelf, Milo Manara, Vittorio Giardino, Durk Dehner and Sharon at the Tom of Finland Foundation, Nick Bertozzi, Tony Bennett at Knockabout and Hunt Emerson, John A Short and Neil Aldis at *Men Only* for *Brit Starr* permissions. Andreas C. Knigge and Ralf König, John Freeman, Nick Abadzis, Donna Barr, Roberta Gregory, Joe Phillips and Ron McFee, Winston Leyland at Leyland Publications, Steve MacIsaac, Scott Lewis, Jason Atomic, Barry Blair and Colin Warbridge, Howard Chaykin, Harris Miller, Bryan Talbot, Patrick Fillion, Kev O'Neill, Dave Gibbons, Oliver Frey, Phil Foglio, Frank Cho, Spain Rodriguez, Scott Dunbier, David Shenton, Stan Shaw, John Higgins, Garry Leach, Fredrik Stromberg, Junko Mizuno, Gengoroh Tagame, Mike and Cassandra Conroy, Jess Fink, Simon Bisley, Thierry Plée at Tabou Editions, Robert Triptow, Tanino Liberatore, Jacques Boivin, Craig McDonald at Verotik, Larry Welz, John Maybury, Jimmy Palmiotti, Amanda Conner, Paul Mounts, Mal Coney and Sean Doran, Ron Hussey, Steve Emond, Phil Jimenez, Craig Hamilton, Tim Vigil, Jordi Bernet and Manuel Auad at Auad Publishing, and all the other countless artists, creators, and publishers who took time out to talk to me, correct my mistakes, offer encouragement, and give permission to reprint your wonderful work. Particular thanks to Garth Ennis for always being a trooper and a good friend.

To my old housemate Will Morgan at 30th Century Comics, London for the loan of key gay comix, and a massive cheers to Howard Cruse for the amazing art, fact-checking, and support.

Bill Storie, Stephanie Johnson, and Mike Rhode for last minute scanning duties.

Thank you to Joseph Melchior for the loan of his Dave Stevens originals and for being a true mate, and to John Bamber for the Paolo Seperi sketch and for smoothing the way with so many people.

A big thanks to Adam, Julie, and Emily for putting up with my constant arguments and prima donna ways, and to Katie Greenwood, Tamsan Barratt, and Sean Wilson for their efficient and diligent additional picture and permissions research.

To Eric Himmel and Charlie Kochman at Abrams for their unwavering support and friendship. Huge apologies to anyone I've missed out.

This book has caused more hurt and pain that I could have ever expected and to those of you who were embarrassed, enraged, dismayed, or offended by this book then I am truly sorry. It was never my intention to cause any distress to anyone, but merely to record an unwritten history of a subgenre of comics. It appears that they are still a very potent source of controversy and animosity.

While writing this book we lost three comic book greats, my old friend Steve Whitaker, Will Elder and Dave Stevens. Steve was a sensational artist, raconteur, colorist on *V for Vendetta* and *New Adventures of Hitler*, and big-hearted man who taught me so much. I miss him. I have been an admirer of *The Rocketeer* creator Dave Stevens's fantastic work since the late eighties. I was kindly granted permission to reprint Will Elder's work in *Erotic Comics* volume one, not long before he passed away. The world will be a lot poorer without their creative geniuses.

Right:
This illustration, *Tag Dis*, was created for a hip-hop magazine by Vaughn Bode's son Mark, who has carried on his father's tradition of erotic comics, as well as becoming a tattooist and designer.